FROM DORSET

Edited by Emma Marsden

First published in Great Britain in 2000 by
YOUNG WRITERS
Remus House,
Coltsfoot Drive,
Woodston,
Peterborough, PE2 9JX
Telephone (01733) 890066

All Rights Reserved

Copyright Contributors 1999

HB ISBN 0 75431 826 5
SB ISBN 0 75431 827 3

FOREWORD

This year, the Young Writers' Future Voices competition proudly presents a showcase of the best poetic talent from over 42,000 up-and-coming writers nationwide.

Successful in continuing our aim of promoting writing and creativity in children, our regional anthologies give a vivid insight into the thoughts, emotions and experiences of today's younger generation, displaying their inventive writing in its originality.

The thought, effort, imagination and hard work put into each poem impressed us all and again the task of editing proved challenging due to the quality of entries received, but was nevertheless enjoyable. We hope you are as pleased as we are with the final selection and that you continue to enjoy *Future Voices From Dorset* for many years to come.

CONTENTS

        Kimberley Huggens   1

Corfe Hills School
- Adam Tilson   1
- Benjamin Sorrell   2
- Laura Sutton & Rachel Payne   2
- Tory Copelin   3
- Duncan Athol   3
- Chanelle Salisbury   4
- Benjamin Stanley   4

Dorchester Middle School
- Joe Gower   5
- Demelza Smith   5
- Adam Jones   6
- Jamie Beasley   6
- Laura Barton   7
- Liam Coward   7
- Abby Gilbert   8
- Toni Holland   8
- Daniel Edwards   9
- Christopher Griffiths   9
- Laurel Burn   10
- Fiona Ball   10
- Sam Napper   11
- Mark Coleman   12
- Jessica Harding   12
- Lisa Hopkins   13
- Beth Downes   13
- Louise Barton   14
- Laura Ballard   14
- Chloe Musgrove   15
- Michelle Baggott   15
- Helen Nicholson   16
- Ryan Cottrell   16
- Kelly Smith   17

Andrea Whitbread	17
Hannah Willsher	18
Angela Bagwell	18
Elizabeth Crawford	19
Nathaniel Shaw	20
Heidi Greatrex	20
James Balls	21
James Lee	21
Michelle Drew	22
Bobby James	22
Tim Graham	23
Rebekah Woodward	23
Jessica Cutler	24
James Nutt	24
Victoria Beames	25
Tom Jackson	25
Zak Grindle	26
Kate Pullin	26
Luke Williams	27
Natasha Legg	27

Parkstone Grammar School

Rhianon Greenslade	28
Sarah Griffin	28
Claire Hill	29
Claire Coombes	30
Helen Samuels	30
Rachel Wall	31
Katie Burden	31
Rianne Davies	32
Carly Fenn	32
Rachel Tucker	33
Sarah Liddiard	34
Hannah Lewis	34
Lucy Martin	35
Hannah Golightly	36
Lydia Mizon	36
Sophie Cross	37

Mei Xuan Lye	38
Anna Sharp	38
Jennie Ewbank	39
Sarah Barker	40
Lucy Mackenzie	40
Alice Dale	41
Laura Goudge	42
Sarah Sweatland	43
Kirsti Pawlowski	44
Vikki Mitchell	44
Sarah Pryor	45
Kitty Bennett	45
Lianne Clark	46
Emma Hawksworth	46
Sarah Baker	47
Vickie Chutter	48
Zoe Anderson	49
Sarah Harvey	50
Rowena Thomas	51
Halina Hickford	51
Rebecca Fewings	52
Amanda Avis	53
Jennifer Turner	54
Debbie Chakrabarti	54
Sharon Brook	55
Jenny Moyse	56
Sam Baldwin	57
Katie Hammond	58
Danika Coghlan	59
Chloé Burden	59
Beejal Parekh	60
Sarah Buckley	60
Teresa Meadows	61
Ella Voce	62
Cathy Jones	63
Sophie Hickman	64
Susanna Marsden	64
Lauren Heaver	65

Claire Wilkinson	66
Lauren Macklin	66
Laura-Jane Neilson	67
Fran Grainger	68
Emily Graham	68
Amy Shepherd	69
Hannah Cumming	69
Kate Atkinson	70
Sophie Mirza	71
Amy Riddell	72
Charlotte Hogg	73
Karen Dance	74
Leanne Cave	75
Lucy Sandford	76
Shelley Richardson	77
Rachel Schmieder	78
Elizabeth Lever	79
Clare Hickman	80
Stephanie Butler	80
Sarah Lings	81
Becky Sykes	82
Helen Davey	82
Laura Greany	83
Sarah Nathaniel	84
Cherilee Real	84
Gemma Knill	85
Mandy Toop	86
Manpreet Aujla	86
Becky Whing	87
Hannah Gilbert	88
Steph Sansome	88
Jessie Jamieson	89
Tegan Palmer	90
Kerry Shea	90
Charlotte Ferguson	91
Jessica Elkin	91
Sían Horan	92
Emily Bustard	92

Marianne Waite	93
Naomi Makiola	93
Susi Berry	94
Laura Wicks	94
Lucie Crew	95
Rachel Faulkner	96
Amy Hebditch	97
Kay Holmes	98
Felicity Quick	98
Jodie Booth	99
Lauren Dyson	100
Susan De Lorey	100
Laura Annis	101
Bridget Keely	102
Sophie Payne	102
Georgina Lang	103
Laura Culham	103
Rebecca Lever	104
Hayley Morris	104
Lauren Bridle	105
Hannah Jeneson	105
Kelly Stark	106
Claire Sissons	106
Gemma Eastman	107
Sally Campion	108
Sophie Clark	108
Jennifer Atkins	109
Natasha Williams	110
Jessica Jarvis	110
Jessica Boize	111
Clare King	112
Kate Kipling	112
Jessica Have	113
Hayley Russell	114
Katie Smith	114
Michelle Cousins	115
Emma Thompson	116
Carissa de Souza	116

Nicola Wall	117
Rebecca Brickwood	118
Rebekah Chadwick	119
Holly Sibley	120
Samantha Wynn-Adams	121
Sarah Belcher	121
Zoe Hyett	122
Lynsey Treharne	122
Ellena Humphries	123
Stephanie Jones	124
Lizzie Paddick	124
Carita Challands	125
Lauren Darby	126
Polly Smith	126
Margaret Goymer	127
Andrea Holmes	128
Katie Merchant	128
Emma Jane Waring	129
Sarah Lonsdale	130
Melissa Hards	130
Lucy Moseley	131
Rosanagh Besley	132
Gemma McCready	132
Kelly Taylor	133
Harriet Archer	134
Helen Gardner	134
Lauren Orchard	135
Heather Marchment	136
Kim Smith	137
Liz Ford	138
Clare Sepping	139
Sian Swift	140

Poole Grammar School

Christopher Howard	140
David Loader	141
Oliver Williams	142
Michael Bannard	143

Tim Matthews	144
Vincent Geoghegan	145
Daniel Wallbridge	146
Peter Hodges	146
Ben Priest	147
Joe Abreu	148
Jonathan Morse	149
Stephen Moore	150
William Hanmer-Lloyd	150
Max Walker	151
Matthew Revill	152
Stephen Worth	153
Daniel Ambrose	154

St Leonard's Middle School, Blandford Forum

Natalie MacDonald	154
Kaylee Hawley	155
Andrew James	156
Claire Stickley	156
Natasha Cox	157
Sam Goudie	158
Natasha Strevens	159

Sherborne School For Girls

Henny Clarke-Hall	159
Katharine Jacob	160
Sophie Byrne	160
Caroline Franklin	161
Lizzy Lillington	162
Fenella Kerr	162
Charlotte Carlton	163
Sarah Hatherell	164
Amy Mayhew	164
Lucy Stewart-Richardson	165
Eleanor Wilson	166
Harriet Crabb	166
Kate Boughey	167
Harriet Gabbey	167

Katie Grimshaw	168
Sara Gledhill	169
Rebecca Wicker	170
Jessica Filbey	170
Jemima Lofts	171

Sturminster Newton High School
Jack Pritchard	172
Gavin Blackhall	173
Ian Lyster	174
Natalie Snook	174
Tiffiny Errington	175
Michelle Dennett	176
Terri-Marie Bugler	176
Sarah Gray	177
Kelly Dowding	178
Keeley Brand	179

The Poems

FRIENDSHIP

A friend is like a candle,
Shining through the night,
Someone you can laugh with,
And share your growing light.

Rainfall in the desert,
Relief through hard times gone,
A shoulder you can cry on,
And teach you right and wrong.

Black ink on white paper,
Contrasting lives to learn,
The exploration of a strange, new world
And selfish thoughts to burn.

Friendship is a lesson,
To tutor how to live,
Guidance in the knowledge that
It's the best thing you can give.

Kimberley Huggens

A FRESH START

I can't wait to see what the future has in store,
Please oh please do not bring more war.
Please bring happiness and wealth, and give
people homes.
Don't make people around the world moan.

If you do all this everyone will be happy,
They'll clean the world, it won't be so scrappy.
I hope there'll be gas and electric powered cars,
So the world won't end, we won't have to live in Mars.

Adam Tilson (13)
Corfe Hills School

SEWAGE!

Sewage floating on the water,
Riding in and out with the tide,
Beaches surrounded by used tissue
And waste driven upon the shoreline.

Sewage has devastating effects,
On fish, plants and human life,
It causes disease and contamination,
Wherever it finds its way to lie!

What are we going to do about it?
This sewage on our shoreline.
If we acted now,
The future will be, just fine.

Benjamin Sorrell (13)
Corfe Hills School

ANIMAL TESTING

People in science labs think it OK,
To take an animal's life away.
Rabbits, rats and little creatures,
Are the scientist's main features.

No matter how hard protesters try
The scientists will always deny
They'll say that the animals are all fine
But really that species will decline.

Laura Sutton & Rachel Payne (13)
Corfe Hills School

SUMMARISING ME

I'm a teenage wonder,
A brain on legs,
I never stop talking,
So my father says.
I like my music,
Full of bass and loud,
I'm not a good dancer,
I stand out in a crowd.
I like the sciences,
I wanna be a vet,
Straight A grades,
Is what I'm going to get.
Netball is my game,
Shooting is my aim,
If I miss a goal
I'll try again.
This isn't a poem,
This is a rap,
My mum says . . .
I can't say that.

Tory Copelin (14)
Corfe Hills School

FUTURE VOICES

I can't wait to see what the future holds for me.
I am going into a new millennium now,
So there is no looking back for me.
Let the millennium people all bind together,
To stop poverty and general snobbery.
But the one thing I wish is to live in peace,
But some people just aren't content with this.

Duncan Athol (13)
Corfe Hills School

LOVE LIFE

L ife is a great thing, you never know what it will bring,
O thers may try to put you down, but you must believe in yourself.
V ery special things happen every day to everyone, but
                                         do they really appreciate it?
E very minute of every day, is special, to someone in every way.

L ove life, enjoy life, live it to the full, enjoy every minute.
I sn't it wonderful the way things happen.
F ull of excitement and sadness that's what life's about,
E very day in every way it's getting better!

   Enjoy life.

Chanelle Salisbury (13)
Corfe Hills School

MY PET DOG

My pet dog is extremely mad,
But I was very glad,
When I got a cat from a tree
That was stuck,
Really I needed a lot of luck.
My guinea pig has a lot of hair,
They get quite lonely so they came in a pair.
My fish, I had not for a long time,
In all I had about twenty-nine.

Benjamin Stanley (13)
Corfe Hills School

SHARKS

The great white shark has big jaws,
When he spots you he doesn't pause.

The whale shark, is the biggest of its kind
But they are hard to find.

The grey shark is quite small
But he is not a fool.

There is a shark with a hammer-head
He searches for food on the seabed.

The basking shark is very kind
It eats on plants which it finds.

All of the sharks live on the seabed
Some of them kill you by biting off your head.

Joe Gower (11)
Dorchester Middle School

THE DARK

Lying in my bed at night,
Clumps and bumps give me a fright.

Shadows move across the wall,
The ghouls and goblins seem very tall.

What is happening to my room
'Cause it is full of doom and gloom?

Demelza Smith (11)
Dorchester Middle School

WHEN YOU'RE IN BED IN THE DARK

Fear
It's under your Titanic bed,
It's in your wooden drawers,
It's just going, going to get you.

It's in your frightening dreams,
It's under your multicoloured covers,
It's just going, going to get you.

It's creaking the dusty stairboards,
It's moving through your gigantic toys,
It's just going, going to get you.

It's in your smelly mysterious bathroom,
It's in your sister's old doll's house,
It's just going, going to get you.

It's moving quicker, quicker,
It's screeching across the floor,
It's just going, going to get you.

Adam Jones (11)
Dorchester Middle School

THE CREEPY HAIRY SPIDER POEM

Slowly creeping around the house,
Peering from behind the cellar door,
Incy-Wincy up the drainpipe,
Daring to crawl across my pillow,
Enjoy wet places,
Run in and out of cracks,
Smack - they're dead!

Jamie Beasley (12)
Dorchester Middle School

GREAT WHITE SHARK

His tummy is white, his back is grey,
His jagged teeth are going to eat you today.
He lies down on the sandy sea floor,
Ready to jump up to eat you some more.

He swiftly swims upon a poor innocent child,
The child doesn't stand a chance, he's too weak, too mild.
The shark swallows him whole in two shark bites,
The child kicks, he screams, he spits and fights.

If I ever encounter a great white shark,
I'll be ready to hit him so he swims like a spark,
He's scarier than a lot of lightning,
I'm sure the experience will be dreadfully frightening.

Laura Barton (11)
Dorchester Middle School

SPIDERS

An eight legged beast
Crawling, sprawling,
Up the wall
Lean, mean
And tall.

Tonight
My mum will survive
The sight, the fright
And live through
The treacherous, terrifying night.

Liam Coward (11)
Dorchester Middle School

Why Do We Need?

Why do we need teachers?
They always tell you off,
You always hear their nails
When they're running out of chalk.
They always bite your head off
When you start to talk.
Why do we need teachers?

Why do we need parents?
They always tell you off,
They tell you to clean your bedroom,
Because they can't do the job.
They tell you to do this,
They tell you to do that,
Why do we need parents?

Why do we need teachers?
They make you want to snore,
They are as bad as your parents,
What do we need them for?

Abby Gilbert (13)
Dorchester Middle School

Spiders

Spiders they're all around you
They're crawling up the wall.
They're up on the ceilings,
Under your bed, in the drawers and
In your bed, in the toy box, in your pillow,
In the bath and under your sink.
They will crawl out of nowhere.

Toni Holland (11)
Dorchester Middle School

My Cat

I have got a cat
That lives in my house.
Its favourite dream
Is to catch a mouse.

She spends all day sleeping
Curled up in the chair.
She is big and fluffy
With long grey hair.

But when she is awake
She likes to play
She attacks my ankles
During the day.

With playing and eating
And plenty of sleep
Our little cat
Is easy to keep.

Daniel Edwards (11)
Dorchester Middle School

Storms

A storm is a wonderful sight,
It brings you a sky full of light;
Always happens in the night which brings a very big fright;
Some say God's switching his lights on and off,
While others just enjoy the night.

Christopher Griffiths (11)
Dorchester Middle School

CLOUDS

I lay on my back in the garden,
Stared up into the misty, blue sky,
Sipped my coke till all was gone
And watched the clouds go by.

They made a lot of funny shapes,
Cats, gerbils and puffing trains,
I like clouds an awful lot,
But not when it rains.

They go all grey and gloomy,
Angry and envious, I know,
But when they decide to pour down,
I know it's time to go.

Inside I remembered that joke about clouds,
At a cricket match, needing the loo,
They couldn't hold on so disaster struck,
Match abandoned for me and you.

Then lots of colours came out in the sky,
Red, orange, yellow and green,
The sun and rain had come together,
A rainbow - that's what I'd seen.

Laurel Burn (12)
Dorchester Middle School

FAMILY

Oh no they're here!
They're getting near!
I'm getting weak at the knees,
'Hello Uncle Cyril and Aunty Rees.'
She's puckering up,
She's ready.

No, no don't
Yuk! I'm going to be sick!
I'll never live it down . . .
The monstrous sloppy smmoch.

Fiona Ball (11)
Dorchester Middle School

FEAR

I am lying in my bed,
The rain is hitting the window,
Thunder and lightning shooting down,
It makes me shake all over my body.
The bed starts creaking
And the floorboards are moving,
I start to sweat,
My body goes cold,
I can't move
I'm frozen with fear!

I am soon asleep
And dream about lions
The lion runs fast
Towards me.
Growling fiercely
I stop suddenly
My heart beats quickly,
My skin looks white and pale
I shudder and wake up
It is completely dark
And very frightening.
The feeling of fear
Is very scary.

Sam Napper (11)
Dorchester Middle School

A KITTEN'S THOUGHT

She sits in the window,
With her eyes open wide,
If only she could go outside,
But she's only a kitten.
Too young to go far,
But she thinks
Just you wait,
I'll soon be out there,
Out in the long grass,
Just waiting for a fat mouse to pass.
Hello!
What's this?
My food!
Has it come at last?
My trip can wait another day.

Mark Coleman (12)
Dorchester Middle School

SHADOW MONSTER!

In the dark shadows
Of the depths beneath
Lurks the shadow monster
Getting ready to eat
He comes up at night
Making a terrible fright
Then he goes back home to
Sleep!

Jessica Harding (11)
Dorchester Middle School

LOVE

I saw a boy
he looked at me,
I looked back
at him beautifully.
We stared and stared,
all day long,
until I realised
I was wrong.
I looked behind me
I saw a girl
and then my head
was in a twirl
and then I decided
to refrain,
from looking at boys,
ever again.

Lisa Hopkins (12)
Dorchester Middle School

ICEBERG

The mountainous polished palace,
Rose vastly above the mighty waves.
A giant snowball plods heavily around,
Like a huge fur coat.
Stranded princess with a silver ball gown on,
A glistening pearl on a golden ring.
It's a pallid swan drifting calmly by.
Sparkling stars dart around in the icy water.

Beth Downes (11)
Dorchester Middle School

WINTER MONTHS

It is cold and gloomy
Snowdrops fall out of the sky.
People say it is cold out here,
People go inside to the warm.
To have a cup of hot cocoa.

Children outside playing in the snow,
Some are building snowmen,
Some are having snowball fights,
Adults calling them and saying,
'It's far too cold to play.'

Christmas is just around the corner,
Children getting very excited,
People kissing under the mistletoe,
Christmas decorations up in the house.
People say *'Merry Christmas everyone
And a happy New Year!'*

Louise Barton (13)
Dorchester Middle School

MONSTER

My bed is full of monsters,
Only I hate to think it,
Not even my mum believes me,
Some are big and some are small,
Terrible things them monsters,
Every night I'm frightened of going to bed,
'Really Laura' my mum said.

Laura Ballard (11)
Dorchester Middle School

THE WEREWOLF

In a full blue moon on a howling night,
On top of a hill there's a werewolf in sight,
Camping in the woods on your own tonight,
When you enter your tent, you can't sleep tonight.

You can hear his victims scream,
You think oh how that beast is mean,
You really hope that isn't you,
When you enter your tent, you can't sleep tonight.

You can hear his paws
And dribbling jaws,
When you enter your tent, you can't sleep tonight,
Will you wake up in the morning
Or will it still be night?

Chloe Musgrove (11)
Dorchester Middle School

GHOST GIRL

The pale young girl got in the taxi
Chatted away till she got home
The driver went to help her out
But when he looked there was nowt.

He decided to check she was alright
The confused mother said 'She died five
Years ago in the night.'
She had been hit by a car
And so the girl had been trying to get
Home ever since,
But never ever succeeded.

Michelle Baggott (12)
Dorchester Middle School

THE FOX

Creeping, crawling in the dark
Always waiting, always watching
For just the right moment
Suddenly he pounces
Stops short with nothing
And slinks back into the shadows.
Waiting, watching, willing
To take just the smallest life.
Like a killer ready to stab
With its knife.
Its poor prey falls to its death,
Not a squeak, not a peak at its killer.
The fox.

Helen Nicholson (11)
Dorchester Middle School

THE SPIDER

The spider is a fearsome creature
Small, fat and shadowy features.
It creeps around in the dark, but doesn't bite,
It could give you a fright.

It makes its web above your head
But never goes under the bed
It lurks around in the damp
And in your bathroom makes it's camp.

Ryan Cottrell (11)
Dorchester Middle School

My Family

Dad is always in a stress
Always over a little mess.
He must be deaf or simply crazy
He always says we are lazy
And when it comes down to Mum
Some people think an angel has come
An angel from hell.
Yes, maybe
They won't even let us watch TV
Oh yes,
My darling bro,
An insane devil even so
And last but by no means least,
Oh yes, it's me.
Beautiful, intelligent and full of modesty.

Kelly Smith (13)
Dorchester Middle School

Cats

They watch and wait
at the garden gate
eyes open and bright
as you see them at night.

They quietly creep
when you're asleep
they make you jump
with their great furry lump
and land on your lap.

Until you clap
and then silently walk away.

Andrea Whitbread (11)
Dorchester Middle School

THE NIGHT

As the daylight fades
And the skies grow black.
I huddle indoors
As all my fears come back.

I draw the curtains
And switch on the light.
To keep the shadows outside
At this time of night.

What was that noise
Out in the yard?
I'll try to be brave
But it's ever so hard.

The night's seem long
Frightening and cold.
I remember all the ghost stories
That I've ever been told.

I'll climb into bed
And set my alarm.
When I wake in the morning
I'll have come to no harm.

Hannah Willsher (11)
Dorchester Middle School

DOLPHINS

See the dolphins jumping through the sea
here for you and here for me.

They swim along with the ships
so the crewmen take a dip.

Hear the dolphins screech and scream
while we're standing on the beach.

Once again, they swim through the sea
here for you and here for me.

Angela Bagwell (12)
Dorchester Middle School

A PERFECT WORLD

I have a dream . . . of a perfect world.
Everyone is happy and smiling,
Flowers don't wilt and die,
The sun rises, but does not set,
People laugh, but do not cry.
There is no such thing as disease,
The animals freely roam,
The sky is always sparkling blue,
Every child has a home.
The birds are always singing,
There is no such thing as war,
There are no greedy people among us,
And so we never ask for more.
Equality is all around us,
Music is always played,
Every plant is gleaming green,
And every sea a glistening jade.
Pollution does not exist,
I wallow in warm sunbeams,
Friends last forever,
And I will always have a dream.

Elizabeth Crawford (13)
Dorchester Middle School

SPIDERS

One night when I went to bed
I saw a gigantic shadow on my bedspread.
I then saw what it was, it was like my worst nightmare had come true.
There was an enormous, hairy spider in my shoe.

Suddenly my eyes went blurred and it felt like I was about to black out,
It then moved ever so close and boy did I shout.
It was getting closer, then suddenly it shot up into the air,
Should I follow it? Would I dare?

All of a sudden I felt some legs sticking into my back
It was like someone had hit my back like a smack.
The creature then came up on to my head
Then I knew it was lying on my bed.

I brushed through my hair
But I could see that it was still there.
My dad then came along to see what was there
And scared it away with his stare.

Nathaniel Shaw (11)
Dorchester Middle School

THE DOLPHIN AND ME

Calm, peaceful, the dolphin glides through the sea
Of waves clear blue, puts trust in me.

Eye to eye we solemnly convene
The waves crash, shimmering green.

As I stand on the beach he swiftly turns -
Go, be free.
Never again the dolphin I will see.

Heidi Greatrex (12)
Dorchester Middle School

DETENTION

Once again I'm in detention
I wasn't paying any attention.
How was I supposed to know
My teacher was watching me jeer my foe?

Once again I'm in detention
Please show just a little affection.
It wasn't me who threw the pen
Across the room at the girl called Jen
Just because it was labelled with my name
It doesn't mean I should take the blame.

Detention is like my second home
That's why I was told to write this poem
And there my story comes to an end
My life's in detention, it's round the bend.

James Balls (12)
Dorchester Middle School

NIGHT-TIME

The darkness fell very fast,
The shadows were getting bigger,
The wind blew with loud whistles
The great big tree had branches crashing.
All the time the shadows were growing
I thought I heard footsteps
I started running
My heart beat faster
A light flashed
I was so afraid.

James Lee (12)
Dorchester Middle School

MY FAMILY

My brother is a total pain,
I think he's really quite insane,
My mum is really nice to me,
Just the way a mum should be.
My dad is out at work all day,
When he comes home, he will say,
'Loads more work,' moan, moan, moan,
'Now I'll have to work at home.'
My gran spoils me and makes a fuss,
And is always giving gifts to us.
My family is not particularly strange.
There's nothing here that I could change.

Michelle Drew (12)
Dorchester Middle School

THE SPIDER

I turned over in my bed
A spider up above my head
In the light, he looked so scary
His body was so hairy.

I lay there very still
He made me feel quite ill,
I tried to pretend I didn't care
Until he dropped upon my hair.

I was out of bed and down the stairs
You would think he was a grizzly bear!

Bobby James (12)
Dorchester Middle School

DINOSAUR DAY

I wish I was a dinosaur, big and mean,
I'd search for animals nice and lean.

Oh, I wish I'd been a dinosaur,
Who would let out an ear splitting roar.

I'd roam around and stamp my feet,
I wouldn't care what to eat.

A nice Diplodocus long and plump,
I'd wait in the bushes, then pounce and jump.

As my teeth sank it, it would cry out in pain,
Then fall to the ground, it was slain.

All the smaller dinosaurs would get out of my way,
'Cos I'm a Tyrannosaurus, and I'm having my day.

Tim Graham (12)
Dorchester Middle School

RATS

The rat . . . emerging cautiously,
from the stench of the dirty sewers.
Its slanted deep red eyes beckon in the darkness,
thick black fur encrusted with germs from the plague.
It appears out of nowhere,
stretching its razor sharp claws,
ready to kill its prey,
the long, slimy tail sways,
as the rat gnaws away,
certainly more vermin will follow.

Rebekah Woodward (12)
Dorchester Middle School

THE FIRE

Fire, fire, burning bright
Warming me up on a cold winter's night.

Yellow, orange, red and gold are the
Colours of the flickering flames.

Licking around the logs and grate,
Crackling and sparkling among the coals.

Pulling my chair up close,
I can feel the warmth through my wriggling toes,
I drift off to a light sleep.

The fire is a gentle glow and glimmer of red,
Lead me to the logs and coal and I will feed,
The fire is its magical yellow and red
The flames can once again leap and dance in the grate,
On this cold winter's night.

Jessica Cutler (11)
Dorchester Middle School

THE KOMODO DRAGON

His swift side winding legs
Moving all over the place
With his scaly brunette skin, this huge creature
Happens to show a wonderful feature,
In sight of a meal, he shows no fear in his face.

His long, lingering tongue,
He follows the trail to become the dominant male
And uses his scent of smell after his dinner is done.

James Nutt (11)
Dorchester Middle School

THE STALKER

Slinking through the long grass
Swishing his tail faster and faster
Going to the pond
Thinking his luck is in tonight.
Will he catch one?
Will he not?
I think not.
Eyes like diamonds
A swipe like a bear
Teeth like needles
I won't go near,
Wrecking the place
With claws like pins
Annoying noise
Prr, prr, prr.
Terrorising the neighbour's dog.
Walking high upon the wall
Taking his daily prowl
Spots Mr Starling
And greets him with a growl
And stalks the mice down below.

Victoria Beames (12)
Dorchester Middle School

RAGS

My dog Rags has got lots of hair,
He's unique - not one of a pair,
He's top at agility,
Full of ability,
A dog with exceptional flare.

Tom Jackson (12)
Dorchester Middle School

I'M A NUTTER

I'm a nutter
Life is so jolly
Dancing around Tesco's
I'm off my trolley.

Help! Help!
I'm off my nut
I'm insane
And I've lost my brain.
Being loopy is not so bad
It's easy being barking mad.

Zak Grindle (11)
Dorchester Middle School

NIGHT

Night is the time when you sit and remember,
Memories of time gone by.
Wearing a dark cloak studded with silver,
Made by the stars in the sky.

Night is the time when the world is the creatures,
Walking the soft dewy grass,
Luminous eyes pierce through the darkness,
Soft footpaws gently tread a path.

Kate Pullin (12)
Dorchester Middle School

Light

At dusk the sun pierces through,
The purple wash of the night,
With orange scattered by
And the wave of the harvested wheat,
Shines in the golden light.
As night draws in, the stars come out
And make a shower of beautiful silver light,
Cascading over the sky.
Like a sweeping sheet.
At dawn, light slowly regains,
Shining through the darkness.
Birds start singing in gracious chorus.
Dew drops off the grass, while the mist lifts,
Day is here once again.

Luke Williams (12)
Dorchester Middle School

The Flight

The plane speeds along the runway,
Then zooms up into the sky.
You are forced back against your seat,
You cling hard onto the arms.
Your ears start to pop,
Wanting but unable to look out of a window.
The sick feeling inside your stomach,
Then all is calm for the moment,
You dream of your destination.

Natasha Legg (11)
Dorchester Middle School

A Tree

A tree is a home to all animals,
So tall and grand it stands,
Its prickly bushes,
Its elegant hands,
Its generous arms give a shelter.

Its colour, so green with envy,
Its branches a musical box,
Its claws clench into the ground, so it stands,
The only movement,
A sway from the breeze.

It sways in the wind,
From dawn till dusk,
Like it were rocking a baby
And the birds they adore this generous creature,
So peaceful, so quiet, so strong.

Rhianon Greenslade (12)
Parkstone Grammar School

She

She sits alone thinking of things to come
Or what it would have been like if things were different.
She wishes for happiness but no smile appears on her face,
Her little blue eyes fill with tears.
She feels scared and confused
Staring into the bright sky,
Wondering.
She remembers her life full of happy, cheerful thoughts
Only a year ago.
Perhaps things could change but for now
She is still alone and scared, waiting.

Sarah Griffin (14)
Parkstone Grammar School

BESIDE THE SEA

The sun is arriving,
Birds fly in.
Waiting for their feeder,
To come.

The calm water ripples,
All is still.
Only birds are moving,
That's all.

Finally they get here,
The food, yum!
Lots of people coming,
At last!

Kids are running wild,
Slap on the cream.
Building up the castles,
So tall.

The fun has nearly ended,
Food's everywhere,
Everybody's leaving.
They've gone.

Paradise has ended,
Not for long,
Birds are starting cleaning,
For more.

Claire Hill (12)
Parkstone Grammar School

COUNTRYSIDE FREEDOM

Sparkling rays of sunlight penetrate out from the fluffy mist of white,
Bending, the fields of dandelions sway gracefully in the spring wind,
Wild freedom lurks throughout the desolate, wilderness
                            of the curved landscape,
Vociferous winds howl out hindering, everything that gets in its way.

The dark, dismal clouds block out the phosphorescence in
                            the sapphire sky,
Mother Nature at work by night and by day perfecting
                            the world we thrive in,
Splendid scenery rushes by,
Going down, into the horizon the torch of the world has
                            vanished from sight.

Claire Coombes (12)
Parkstone Grammar School

AUTUMN

The summer princess has been and gone,
Now the autumn queen has just begun,
As she moves from her lair, high up above,
We feel a chill in the air,
Autumn is here.

The autumn queen never has much time,
Perhaps a month or two, and then she must retreat,
To let the winter king find his feet.

She dashes through the parks and woods,
Touching each tree with her orange wand.
Suddenly the world is alive with colour,
Reds, browns, oranges and yellows.

Helen Samuels (13)
Parkstone Grammar School

THE MOON

The patient moon hangs in the still night air,
Watching the world go by.
She witnesses all good and all bad,
Yet her face stays emotionless.
Her quiet round bulk sees all the bad things at work,
Attracted by her silent magic.
In dark she feels comfort whilst among the bright stars,
And the evil is not evil to her.
Once a month, she shows her whole self,
To the sky, the planets, the sun and all stars.
But none of the daytime feel her mysterious power,
They believe that the sun holds the greatest of knowledge.
They are wrong,
They will see,
When she breaks free . . .

Rachel Wall (12)
Parkstone Grammar School

NIGHT

The stars are set in the dark blue sky
And the black night casts its eerie shadow.
The whole world stands still,
The night mist is out;
And all that is heard
Is the distant sound
Of an owl or a scattering mouse.
The moon is resting in the motionless universe
And the trees and birds
Are merely silhouetted shapes
Up against the silver shine of the moon.

Katie Burden (12)
Parkstone Grammar School

THE SEASIDE

There's chaos at the seaside,
Crabs pinching toes,
Sandy sandwiches,
Silly inflatables in the sea.
Grannies and grandpas
Lying in deckchairs
With sunhats
And seaweed.
Building magnificent sandcastles,
Or digging the deepest holes.
Ice-creams galore,
Extravagant picnics
Fascinating rock pools
Screeching seagulls stealing sandwiches
And sand in everything.

Rianne Davies (12)
Parkstone Grammar School

THE RIVER

The river tumbles and falls
Flowing faster as it goes
Passing hills and towns
Bubbling, gushing, swishing, swirling.
Cascading in beautiful waterfalls.
Then, suddenly calm.
The fish swim in its murky depths
Unaware of the power it contains.
Finally the river cascades its last
And reaches the final destination.
The end of all rivers,
The sea.

Carly Fenn (14)
Parkstone Grammar School

THE BLACK CAT

> His long sleek black body,
> and his velvet padded paws,
> with a silky clean fur coat
> and his dazzling green eyes,
> are some of this cat's perfections
> you see when he comes your way.

The elegance of his walk,
the swiftness of his attack,
the graceful way he leaps
and the sheer speed of his run,
are some of this cat's perfections
you see when he comes your way.

> His white hairs are starting to show now,
> his miaow is becoming weaker,
> his attack no longer kills or harms
> for his teeth, they are long gone,
> these are some of this cat's imperfections.
> you see when he comes your way.

The great prince of all the cats
is slowly being beaten down
for he no longer has the energy
to fight, to attack, or to evade,
you no longer see any perfections
when this cat regretfully slinks away.

> His long sleek black body
> and his velvet padded paws,
> with a silky clean fur coat
> and his dazzling green eyes,
> were some of that cat's perfections
> which he now no longer has.

Rachel Tucker (13)
Parkstone Grammar School

BONFIRE NIGHT

The fire burns,
The people gathered round,
Talking of the past.
The noise blends in with the
Cackles, hisses and pops.
The flames leap high into the sky,
Forming pictures of yellow, orange and red
From your imagination.
Casting shadows off the trees,
Like hands reaching out to the crowd,
Drawing them closer to its warmth.
The smoke disappears into the midnight sky,
That is speckled lightly with stars.

Gradually the fire dies,
Leaving embers glowing until dawn.

Sarah Liddiard (12)
Parkstone Grammar School

THE SEASON TREE

The tree sways with the gentle autumn breeze,
The leaves gracefully dancing,
As there falling to the ground,
The autumn leaves are red, orange, brown and amber,
They cover the ground like a carpet,
Leaving the branches free and bare.

The winter now is setting in,
The leaves are starting to cover with frost,
A white layer begins to conceal the tree,
As it freezes in the winter chill.

The snow begins to slowly melt,
It's springtime now
And trees are covered with beautiful blossom,
Pinks, creams and purples,
The birds sing happily,
As they're making nests and laying their eggs.

Their eggs are hatching,
Amongst the bright green leaves,
The tree is now fresh and shining,
Sunbathing under the warm summer sun,
Phew! Wasn't that a busy year.

Hannah Lewis (12)
Parkstone Grammar School

EARTHQUAKE!

Trembling, softly
Shaking, jolting
Buildings
Cars
Fallen and crushed.

People hurt
Homes destroyed
Shaken
Scared
Earthquake has gone.

Light back on
Destruction seen
Shock
Horror
Silence, stillness.

Lucy Martin (12)
Parkstone Grammar School

THE FIFTH OF NOVEMBER

A fire burns on the fifth of November,
It's a night you will always remember
Fireworks explode in the night sky,
Crackling and banging way up high.
On the bonfire the flames seem to fly,
Over the logs and onto the Guy.
The sparklers shimmer and light up the land,
Watched by many, it's oh so grand
Smiling faces, happy grins,
This is where the fun begins!
The glowing embers in the fire,
The fireworks soaring higher and higher
The fun for all to be had,
A night when everyone is glad.
A fire burns on the fifth of November
It's a night you will always remember.

Hannah Golightly (12)
Parkstone Grammar School

SPACE

'Space is the new frontier.'
A whole new way of life,
Waiting, waiting to be discovered.
Brave men risk their lives
To feed our craving for knowledge.
Is there life out there?
Men make promises they cannot keep -
That one day we will know everything
About space.

'Space is the new frontier.'
A risk because it is a mystery,
Lying in wait for its next victims.
Brave men risk their lives
To feed our craving for knowledge.
Is there anything out there?
Men send their brothers into the unknown,
Some never return.
Black holes, asteroids, UFOs.
Space.

Lydia Mizon (13)
Parkstone Grammar School

MOUNTAINS

Mountains are tall and reach the sky . . .
Up to the peak, the birds do fly.
Up in the clouds lots to see,
Looking down on you and me.
Mountains are tall and reach the sky . . .
Oh aren't they high.
Looking up to the sky and down to the ground,
Never a smile and never a frown.
Mountains are tall and reach the sky . . .
I would love to be a mountain,
Looking at everyone and everything.
It could get a bit lonely though,
Up in the sky with no one to talk to.
Mountains are tall and reach the sky . . .
Poor old mountain . . .

Sophie Cross (12)
Parkstone Grammar School

THE OUTSIDER

I watch all the other children
Playing with everyone
I wish I could play with them
But when I come out they are gone.

It's like there's something wrong with me
Like I've got some kind of disease
And no matter how hard I try
They're just too hard to please.

So I've given up trying to please them
Because now I know the truth
You're judged on your colour, skin or race
Things you don't get to choose.

Mei Xuan Lye (13)
Parkstone Grammar School

THE STORM

The howling wind that blows
and the trees swaying to and fro.
Down comes the rain
slashing at the windowpanes.
Lightning strikes
thunder rumbles.
This is where creatures struggle.
Some children squeal with delight
and some squeal with fright.
The wind stops blowing,
the trees stop swaying,
lightning and thunder are no longer playing.

Anna Sharp (12)
Parkstone Grammar School

WHITE HAS THE EDGE

Sitting under a table in the corner of the chemistry lab,
she weeps.
Hiding from the bullies who she has become scared of.

They are no bigger than her,
no older than her,
just a different colour to her.

Her skin is black,
their skin is white,
her hair is black,
their hair is blond.

The thing that scares her,
is how they seem different.
The only thing that gives them the edge,
is being white.

They treat her like an animal,
she lives,
but only in the background,
as though her feelings don't really count.

She isn't the same,
so she's not really there.

She wouldn't swap what she looked like for the world,
but to swap what they looked like,
she would give anything.

She would give anything to be accepted,
for what she is,
not judged by her race or her colour.

Jennie Ewbank (13)
Parkstone Grammar School

Eagle

A daring eagle,
Willing to please.
A lady's man,
Cocksure.
He swoops down, almost touching the long grass,
Then up, high onto the rocky mountains.
He perches,
Still as night.
His gleaming eyes,
Watching,
Watching,
He plumes his feathers.
Then, on sight of prey,
He is off,
Swooping, gliding, cutting through the air,
He is diving,
Closer,
Closer,
Success!

Sarah Barker (12)
Parkstone Grammar School

Music

It's a melodic metaphor,
A trip to your melodic mind.
You hum along,
Trying to stay in time,
There's drones
Melodies,
Ostinatos galore,
And many, many more.

If music is your game
And your only desire.
Then pick up a flute,
Or sing by the fire.
You'll play a crotched,
A quaver,
A crotchet again
Then it will never end!

Lucy Mackenzie (12)
Parkstone Grammar School

FAME

As your debut single goes to number one
All your privacy is ripped away
Every magazine wants an interview
Wherever you go, you are recognised.

There aren't enough hours in the day
Up at five am and bed at one.
With travelling from venue to venue
To the screaming fans you never knew were there.

As you get a second and third number one
You have to learn to keep your feet on the ground,
'Cause people will look up to you
And criticise every mistake.

Eventually your famous glow will fade
And you don't always get to number one
But your loyal fans will stick by you
And for them your glow will never fade.

Alice Dale (13)
Parkstone Grammar School

THE SEASON CIRCLE

The river flowed
The flowers blossomed,
Continually through the summer
Then one day
Autumn came
The season of mass death.

Flowers drooped,
Trees turned bare,
During the long term time
Then one day
Winter came,
The season of the moon.

Snowflakes fell,
Presents unwrapped,
All through the holidays.
Then one day
Spring came
The season of rebirth.

Babies were born
Plants grew
All through the springtime.
Then one day
Summer came,
The season of the sun.

The river flowed,
The flowers blossomed,
Continually through the summer.
Then one day,
Autumn came
The season of mass death.

The circle continues,
Never changing,
It will never change.
Until one day,
Destruction comes,
The seasons will be no more.

Laura Goudge (14)
Parkstone Grammar School

UNCOOL

They spit on me in the playground,
They kick me on the bus.
They said I wouldn't know what hit me,
If I told or made a fuss.
I sit alone in lessons,
They avoid me like the plague.
Only one girl is nice to me,
Her name is Jessy Hague.
Sometimes she sticks up for me,
But they threaten her as well,
I dread it when it's half-past twelve
And I hear the lunchtime bell.
As soon as the teacher's out of sight,
They run after me and start a fight.
I usually hide in the library,
I feel safe in there,
But as soon as I come out,
They shout and pull my hair.

I really can't see anyway out,
I thought of not going to school
And all of this has come to be,
For just not being cool.

Sarah Sweatland (13)
Parkstone Grammar School

SPACE

Alone it stands,
Miles away,
Filled with stars,
Planets and moons.

Away in the darkness,
With stars shining out
The darkness is clear,
The silence is heard.

A land full of galaxies
Each one unknown
Except for one,
Where life has evolved.

Many rockets sent there
Some never return,
And life is lost,
That won't come again.

Kirsti Pawlowski (13)
Parkstone Grammar School

DANDELION

Happy and sad drifting slowly by
In a calm and gentle breeze.
Relaxed and contented,
Magical and warm.

Fluffy and soft,
New seeds flying to a new life.
Time stops to say goodbye
To the wispy fluff.

Vikki Mitchell (13)
Parkstone Grammar School

THOUGHTS

I'm trapped, trapped within my own thoughts.
I cannot escape, there is no way out.
Help! Someone help me, please.
All day long I think, think and think.
Some of these thoughts I don't want to think.
Like sad things and painful things.
Friends I left behind, friends I've never made.
People I knew who've come and gone.
People I'll never know.
These thoughts float round my mind,
All day long, all night long.
I can never escape from my thoughts,
I'm trapped, trapped within my own thoughts.

Sarah Pryor (13)
Parkstone Grammar School

FROZEN

I wake up and look out of my window
Over the fields that were once grey
Now lies a thick sheet of snow.

The icicles hang from my gate
Torn away from their wires
The shadows lie helplessly on the ground.

On the horizon I see a black figure
Not moving, just gazing up at the sky
I wonder, has time frozen too?

Kitty Bennett (13)
Parkstone Grammar School

REJECTION

Looking through the window of society,
Seeing the people,
Knowing I will never be one of them.
I am ignored and shut out,
My existence washed away from all knowledge.

My words are blown away with the wind,
My identity erased,
Like a mistake on a piece of paper.
Seen as nothing,
Never to be acknowledged.

Why are we judged by our race, colour or creed,
And discarded if we aren't right?
Not allowed to be equal,
Unable to be free.

Lianne Clark (13)
Parkstone Grammar School

HE ONLY NEEDS A FRIEND

The lion prowls through the jungle,
Weaving his way through the trees,
Feeling very alone.

The lion prowls through the jungle,
Feeling misunderstood,
Why won't someone be his friend?

The lion prowls through the jungle,
Looking for a mate,
But there is no one around.

The lion prowls through the jungle,
Trying to understand,
For beneath his harsh exterior,
Is a friend waiting to be found.

Despite his snarling mouth,
His deadly claws and his rugged mane,
He's just a sad and lonely cat
Longing to be found.

He means no harm,
Why is everyone scared?
He means no harm,
The lion just needs a friend.

Emma Hawksworth (13)
Parkstone Grammar School

BUTTERFLY

He floats effortlessly through the air,
Every flip and flap.
Gliding along with ease.

Each colour in his gossamer wings
Makes him unique to his kind.
Black, red, yellow, blue, green
Merge together to form a paint box.

Gracefully he flutters past,
Looking for sweet nectar.
Delicate features
Tell-tale of his gentleness.
Fly high little butterfly
Spread your wings for all to admire.

Sarah Baker (12)
Parkstone Grammar School

Disco

We sit excited in the car,
Before the disco,
Before the music,
Before the buzzing ears and headaches.

At home we get dressed,
All talking and giggling,
Exchanging make-up ideas . . .
Just a little apprehensive about how we look.

Eye shadow, eye liner, mascara
They all must go on
Mascara splash on the floor
Eye liner scribbled on the wall.

Tea before anything else
Pizza and chips
Nice and fattening
Our nerves are pouncing.

Half an hour to go
Lipstick, lip gloss, lip liner
We've got to do our nails,
Our hair's still shoved up from school.

In the car . . .
Our hair, nails and face are done,
They all look great
Do I?

In the disco!
It hits you straight away
Boom, boom, boom,
It's so loud, will we ever stop hearing it?

So hot, it's boiling
Like a sauna
I'm so thirsty
I'm so red, but they all look perfect.

In the car
It's 11.30, I can't hear anything
Except a continual
buzzzzzz.

Vickie Chutter (12)
Parkstone Grammar School

THE MOON

The moon,
Skimming softly and silently across the starry sky
Suspended by an invisible thread
Hanging motionless in space.
The pits and craters of its shining face
Illuminated by the silver light
It shines forth on ground.
Large, soft and mysterious.
It proceeds on its journey.
Sinking as the sun begins to rise,
Rising as the sun starts to sink.
The cosmic dance goes on.
The lunar lobe of light lessens as the sun arrives.
Dying softly and slowly with the stars
Shining less and less until
Dawn appears.

Zoe Anderson (13)
Parkstone Grammar School

SPACE

Galaxy after galaxy,
Of lifeless planets,
Waiting to be invaded,
By loudness and evolution.

There's no oxygen to breathe,
Just emptiness to suffocate,
There's no shelter for safety,
Just you to protect yourself.

The planets can't communicate,
They can only glance at each other,
Through the mists of emptiness,
Hoping for life one day.

Silence is heard,
By the ears of the planets,
Which lay undisturbed
In their long living emptiness.

Space continues with nothing to stop it,
To eternity and beyond,
Waiting for something to happen,
Waiting for anything to happen.

The planets have no one,
Our planet has everyone,
The planets have no company,
We have each other for company.

Sarah Harvey (13)
Parkstone Grammar School

THE OUTSIDER

She is always on the outside,
Always looking in,
Waiting for her turn,
That she knows will never come.

She is shy and never confident,
No faith in herself,
Yet always hoping,
That some day she will fit in.

Lonely in her corners,
She is invisible and left out,
But she is resigned to the fact,
That she will never be the same.

How miserable life is,
Why couldn't she be normal?
Instead, fate has made her
An outsider.

Rowena Thomas (13)
Parkstone Grammar School

TIME

The ticking of the clock,
Matches the beating of my heart,
As it works its way through my veins.
Eternity is consumed in a tick
Yet returns in a tock
For without it . . .
There would be chaos.

Halina Hickford (13)
Parkstone Grammar School

ALONE

In the corner of the playground,
The little boy waits alone.
Forgotten by the other children,
Who will never say 'Hello.'

They won't go and talk to him,
Or ask him to come and play,
Because he's not one of them,
He's different, or so they say.

In his eyes the hurt shows
And also a longing untold,
He wants to be one of them,
Not forgotten like days of old.

The children never really care,
That he is on his own.
For below their smiling faces,
There are cold hearts of stone.

The boy is a social outcast,
But he can see,
Because of his colour,
Friends they will never be.

In the corner of the playground,
The little boy waits alone.
Forgotten by the other children,
Who will never say 'Hello.'

Rebecca Fewings (13)
Parkstone Grammar School

OUTSIDE

I look, longingly inside,
Knowing that where that is;
I'm not.

I can't accept that
I'm different
From the rest.

Is it my skin,
My race, belief
Or clothes?

What have I done
To be cast aside?
Just like a dusty toy.

On a shelf.
I stand alone,
Waiting, hoping . . .

I wonder what living
On the inside is like?
I guess I'll never know.

Anger throbs now,
Through my every vein.
Other children's playful teasing:

It's the worst thing
To have to suffer.
I'll continue looking.

Longingly inside I look,
Wishing, waiting,
Hoping . . .

Amanda Avis (13)
Parkstone Grammar School

DO I HAVE TO BE ALONE?

Sitting by the window, alone,
Looking out, I see friends,
Playing, laughing . . . happiness.

I think about other children,
Like me,
Who need a friend to rely on,
Laugh with, trust . . .

What do they do during break?
Do they try and make a friend?
Do they sit and wish they had a friend?

I turn and look at the friends in the playground,
And I see, alone,
A girl sat, alone,
No one to talk with. She was alone.

As I approach her,
She smiles as if to say:
Be my friend, please,
It's never too late to make a friend.

Jennifer Turner (13)
Parkstone Grammar School

THE OUTSIDER

She sat on her own,
at the back of the class.
She faced the wall,
and her head never moved.

When the lessons were over,
and break finally came.
It seemed like a relief,
to everyone, but her.

Silent, she would be,
while others laughed,
stared and teased her.
She was known as the outsider.

When she talked,
she talked just like one of us.
When she smiled,
She smiled just like one of us.

But to be with her,
meant to be one of her.

Debbie Chakrabarti (13)
Parkstone Grammar School

VIOLET

That winter sunset with all its swirling beauty,
The clouds, the sky, the slowly sinking sun.
Leaving trails of colour on the early evening horizon
Leaving traces of the day.

That fruit, so juicy and ripe,
The soft, sweet flesh inside
Oh, how tasty, so delicious,
With a skin looking the same as the sunset.

Those flowers once mentioned to me in an old love poem
That smell, so sweet,
The petals so delicate,
Fragile, soft, scented.

And lastly the wrapper covering, that smooth, desirable chocolate.
Cadbury, it was called.
A glass and a half of full cream milk
Covered in a colour, just as good.

Sharon Brook (13)
Parkstone Grammar School

FOREST FIRES

Deadly,
At the best of times.
Flickering and blazing.
Scary,
Fire; spectacular,
In a dark night sky.
Burning forests,
The revolting smell of petrified wood.
Picturesque beauty dying,
Twisted trees flaming,
Autumn leaves rustling - as if in a hurry to get away.
Water pouring all around,
As the moon watches from above.
Firefighters rushing to save lives,
But many are already dead!
Whole forests disappearing,
Orange flames raging between trees,
Killing,
Slaughtering,
Murdering,
The ultimate *kings of the ground.*

Nothing on Earth can stop it,
A force which humans can't stop.
It's a war!
A losing battle
But so far the penny hasn't dropped,
That,
If we let this go on,
Farmers killing for land,
Our world will die!

It's our future!
It's up to us!
We have to stop the deliberate damage
And,
Prevent forest fires at all costs!

Jenny Moyse (13)
Parkstone Grammar School

TO BE WITH THEM

Outside
Looking in
That's where I am
Standing on the ledge.

I can't get in
Although I'm trying
To be
In there with them.

They don't know me
Why should they?
I'm outside
They're in.

I want to be in there
I really do
I'm having trouble getting there
But I'll get in one day.

One day I'll live their lives
The lives they live today
I'll be living tomorrow
The day they go away.

Sam Baldwin (13)
Parkstone Grammar School

THE OUTSIDER

They see me,
I see them.
I think of how it used to be
With my friends and me.

I'd look at them,
They'd look at me.
We would say 'Hi,'
My friends and I.

I don't talk to them,
They don't talk to me.
I think of how it used to be,
With my friends and me.

I'd talk to them,
And they'd talk to me.
We would do everything together,
Me and Trevor.

I don't do anything with them,
They don't do anything with me.
I think of how it used to be,
My friends and me.

I'd laugh at them,
They'd laugh at me.
This is not how it's supposed to be,
With my friends and me.

They don't want to know me,
But I want to know them.
I wish it was how it used to be,
With my friends and me.

Katie Hammond
Parkstone Grammar School

COLD MOUNTAIN

The snow capped giant stands,
Tall, lonely, cold
Its harsh landscape touched only
By the mountain goat's dainty,
Tiptoeing feet.

Once a proud volcano
Striking fear, terror in people's hearts
He stands a shadow of his former self.

Now many holes gape in his weary face,
From many a hiker's boot,
No more is he mighty.

Danika Coghlan (12)
Parkstone Grammar School

THE RAINBOW!

The bright pastel colours of the rainbow,
Break through the pale, blue morning sky.
Its carefree life projected.
Its happiness transferred to the people below.

Its red is angry and fiery,
Its orange, young and fresh,
The yellow, perfect and shy
And the green crisp and cool.
Also, with its moody yet calm blue.
Next depressing indigo and
Mysterious violet - it shines through our day.

Chloé Burden (12)
Parkstone Grammar School

CLOUDS

As if a living daydream,
All alive in the sky,
Beautiful and fluffy,
Warm and inviting.

Sunshine,
Warmth,
Loving,
And joys,
A wonderful sparkle of emotion:
To enlighten the sky.

It's so there and real,
Yet not there and you will never feel it.
Invisible yet,
Clear, and yet not.

Dainty and strong,
Beautiful as a sunset,
Beautiful as gold,
Lovely as a baby sleeping
And as wondering as love!

Everyone has a silver lining!

Beejal Parekh (12)
Parkstone Grammar School

STEPS UP THE MOUNTAIN

It stands there cold and lonely
Head up in the clouds
Towering, thick and steep.

Most of it has not been touched,
By the footsteps of man
As the mountain goats stagger, trot but stumble,

It can get very cold and
The air gets very
Snowy, unbreathable and frozen.

So as you look from the bottom
As it's towering up above
And you're thinking
'I can climb that,'
Think again, it's a mountain,
It's huge.

Sarah Buckley (13)
Parkstone Grammar School

AUTUMN

It's here again, the autumn time
Leaves are falling, flowers are dying
Crops are being harvested
Wheat, corn, oats and grain.

She's here again with her cursing hand,
Making trees go bare, fields and flowerbeds
But also good things,
Farmers get fed.

She's made the
Days go shorter
Days get colder
Days for the fire burning bright.

Ducks and geese,
And other birds
Go to warmer places
Autumn's here and it's here to stay
Till winter.

Teresa Meadows (12)
Parkstone Grammar School

GIRLS' NIGHT OUT!

I thought the lesson would never end,
It was Friday and so near the weekend,
Tonight was the disco, we'd all been waiting for,
As soon as the bell went, we were all out the door.

When I got home I took a shower
And deciding what to wear took an hour,
Jeans, combats or that little Gucci dress,
Oh my gosh my hair looks a mess.

Which nail varnish goes with this outfit,
No, that cannot be another zit,
Why can't I find socks as a pair
And I still can't figure out what to do with my hair.

Now to pick a pair of shoes,
I have so many I cannot choose,
Almost forgot the mascara and lipstick
And don't tell me I think I've lost my ticket.

What about a jumper in case it gets cold,
Oh no, not that one it's far too old,
Little sis get out of my room,
Is that the time, we should be going soon.

Mum this skirt is not too short
And these shoes are not too high before you give a second thought,
When I arrived I was a bit late,
But in the end it was great.

Ella Voce (12)
Parkstone Grammar School

THE MOON

I am racing to the moon,
and I hear a big caboom!

'What was that?'
It's an alien that's rather fat.

Quick I can almost see the moon
and I want to get there real soon.

Stop the fiery blast,
we're on the moon at last.

As the astronauts climb out,
one of them quickly shouts

'Yuk! What's that cheesy smell?
It doesn't make me feel all that well.'

After that it's time for the flag,
Quickly pick it up, don't let it drag.

In it goes very soundly,
but after that, the silence goes loudly.

Now it's time to taste the cheese,
'Mmmm!' Say a few, 'more please.'

There are some green people over there,
They're looking at us with a stare.

They're trying to communicate, what do we say?
Perhaps we should just run away!

Into the spaceship everyone,
Now it doesn't seem all that fun.

Off we go home again,
Will our story give us fame?

Cathy Jones (12)
Parkstone Grammar School

MY FIRST DAY AT SCHOOL

Shoes all nice and shiny
My socks are new and straight
My shirt does feel funny
Sure I'm gonna be late.

Brand new bag and hairbands
Pencil case and lunch box
Mum is waving her hands
Shouting 'Straighten those socks.'

Drive into school by Dad
'Love you Sophie! Good luck
Hope it isn't too bad'
I'm an outsider, stuck.

Sixth formers stop and stare
Pathetic looks all around
All we can do is glare
Moan like dogs in a pound.

Home time - was that just it?
That was great, I must say
On the bus, down we sit
What a fantastic day!

Sophie Hickman (12)
Parkstone Grammar School

IMAGERY

'Now write a poem on imagery,' the teacher said.
'Imagery?' said we.
'Yes, it's a cool summer breeze on a warm, warm day
And the softness of your bed.
It's the feel of running water
And the smell of fresh cut grass.
It's the colour of ice-cream and the boredom of maths class.'

'But Miss, those are examples, what is imagery?'
'Imagery is the feeling that you're really there!
You can almost smell that lemon.
You could be feeling that breeze from the sea.
You can picture that purple cloud.
You could be hearing those gunshots ring out,
That, child, is imagery!'

Susanna Marsden (12)
Parkstone Grammar School

THE ROSE

Wistfully she stands, looking through the merciless glass,
hoping for the time that never comes.
Craned slender neck, and wilting head is all she has to give.
Rusted petals curling over, retarded by her frame, wondering, but
knowing, that things will never be the same.
Her proud thorns are prickles now, she knows that she is tamed, each
hour, each day, a petal falls, she knows that she is maimed,
No one can answer pleas for help, no one out there can hear, from
within her rich, velvety centre, trickles down a tear.
She longs for the cold, hard rain, to be outside with the others again,
She cannot see her rusted form, but knows the others can, the
whispering hurts, so does the wound.
All blackened, all shrivelled up, a centre for her shame, that cut, that
sharp clean cut, the cut in her stem that takes the blame.
Her prick, her hopes have left her deserted, they soon fled.
Her sweet perfume, goes too, all that's left is her crippled
stick, oh the pain that she bled.
Captured, and dropped into a pretty glass cage, she stands a sorry sight
and here I stop, for pity of her, to end her undignified plight.

Lauren Heaver (12)
Parkstone Grammar School

THE VALLEY

The stone cold river
Trickled peacefully toward the
Deserted space.
At the end of the valley.

All alone - neglected
Still and solemn
This silent setting stands desolate
With only the stiff breeze as company.

It's cool, calm, complexion is merely on the surface
Within the picturesque place
Is an airy open emptiness
Only to be discovered by those who venture.

Shallow minded individuals pass by
Not noticing the hollow scenery
Its ridged edges
And curved sticks.

At nightfall the silence
Echoes the sway of the wind
And the soft unnaturalness of the
Running water erodes the valley away . . .

Claire Wilkinson (13)
Parkstone Grammar School

AUTUMN

There she is just standing there
giving me that stony glare
A lady dressed in brown and yellow,
looking glum and rather mellow.
She makes the leaves die and fall off their trees
scattered around for all to see.

But on the inside of that stony glare,
there's someone in there that really cares.
She loves to see children running about,
enjoying autumn with a laugh and a shout.
Flinging an array of different coloured types of leaves.
Browns, yellows, oranges and sometimes greens.
It'll be sad when she has to go
because next comes the ice and snow.

Lauren Macklin (12)
Parkstone Grammar School

QUEEN OF THE NIGHT

Gradual darkness surrounds the whirling Earth
The navy sky duchess is yet to appear.
Her glistening servants gather,
Shimmering,
Glimmering,
Swarming.

Proudly, graciously
Her immaculate moonlight
Prowls our radiant space
Entering
Her unique
World.

Tonight she is glorious
Glorious as can be
Stencilled craters deepen her knowledge
She is special, as special as
The queen honey bee
For she owns more than honey bee
She owns the *world*.

Laura-Jane Neilson (12)
Parkstone Grammar School

WAR

Bang, bang,
The guns all chant
As the soldiers move forward and the enemy retreats.
The identical army are quick and so brave,
Unaware of the deaths they have caused.
They are merciless in firing and sly in their ways
Always ready to kill.

But how on earth will the enemy feel
With our army never retreating?
They'll peep out from their trenches,
Risk a quick glance
But never move forward, always move back.
But at the end of it all,
Each soldier must know;
How many lives he has wasted?

Fran Grainger (12)
Parkstone Grammar School

SHE STANDS ALONE

An old lady stands alone in this dismal world.
Her fragile face holds a maze of wrinkles.
The smooth apron folds across her withered skin.
Once bright eyes are tired.
The silence she lives in is piercing.
Empty inside her she waits -
Waiting for nothing is a tiresome task.

Her house is a symbol of memories once shared.
A picture of her husband is hung in every room.
He is dead and gone, forever.
An old lady stands alone in this dismal world.

Emily Graham (13)
Parkstone Grammar School

ME

I had a dream,
That I was me.
That's what people say,
I should be.
They say, don't be like Sue
And don't be like Jane
And I try
And I try
But it's all in vain.
My nose is too big,
My feet are too small,
There's nothing about me,
I don't fit in at all.
But I had a dream
And I am me.
That's what I am
And shall always be.

Amy Shepherd (11)
Parkstone Grammar School

SILVER SHIVER

Rustling leaves.
Moss on the trunk.
Golden, shimmer,
Silver, shiver.
Woodpecker's hole.
Owls nest.
Grand, stout trunk.
Cunning, little branches.
A tree.
A forest.

Hannah Cumming (12)
Parkstone Grammar School

My Big Break

Nerves and tension
Were building up inside,
I can't go on
'I can't' I cried.

I checked my script
just once, or twice
I checked my clothing
I did look nice.

I was dressed like a dancer
then to be a maid
and they were only two
of the parts I played.

I'd be on stage for an hour
under the spotlight.
The others in the dark
but I'd be bright.

Five minutes and counting
fear and anticipation
and then I'd be on
and into formation.

Two minutes
my stomach churned
I took a big gulp
and my throat burned.

I can't lose my voice
not here, not now
I'll just keep on speaking
and raise it somehow.

The curtains open
the spotlights on me
I open my mouth
what sound will it be?

A squeak,
but I almost spoke
the audience were silent
this was no joke!

They called my understudy
but her temperature was too hot
and without the main character
it kind of spoils the plot.

Kate Atkinson (12)
Parkstone Grammar School

FIRE

Mesmerising, the
Crackling beast lures
Anyone willing to watch
Willing to watch its claws,
Its talons,
Reaching towards the cold,
Dark sky
Evoking heat, energy
And the blinding brightness.
Illuminating shadows.
Chasing away anything
Unwilling to fall
Beneath its glowing power.

Sophie Mirza (13)
Parkstone Grammar School

UNKNOWN

My hair flew across my face
Flying loose with the wind,
The cool air formed a mould around my face
The face of unknown.

As I walked along the promenade
The wind grew stronger,
Unwrapping the mask
The face of unknown.

People staring, causing pain
Striking down on me,
My heart shredding, ruining
The face of unknown.

'Who are you?' I ask myself
I am no one,
No soul, no life, just
The face of unknown.

I want to be myself
Unwrap the hidden me,
Show everyone who I am and that I'm not just
The face of unknown.

I want to love, hate, be a person
Enter the real world,
I want a friend who will discover
The face of unknown.

Amy Riddell (13)
Parkstone Grammar School

THE MYSTERY COLOUR

It was a bright summer's day
I felt warm and secure, I was
Thinking of wonderful things.
The lovely smell of a rose, and
The joy of nice ripe tomatoes, and
The crunch of rosy apples.

The pleasure of picking fruits
With the sun on my back
Like strawberries and raspberries
And then the joy of eating my fill.
Till I was ready to burst.

As I was wandering down the road,
I saw a post box, bright in the sunlight.
Standing to attention as if on parade.

I came to a traffic light
The top light was shining.
It made me aware,
It shouted *danger! Stop and beware!*

People were lying in the sun.
Their bodies were bright like the colour
Of a lobster.
They will be sorry
And say never again.

At the end of the day
The summer sunset on the horizon
Was the colour of wine.
This poem has made me so happy
I wish it could rhyme.

Charlotte Hogg (12)
Parkstone Grammar School

LIFE

Standing tall and strong
watching the world
pass by,
every move
slow and sturdy
the tree remembers his childhood days.

The young sapling
standing in his mother's shade,
his bending trunk and small branches
that protect him from the storm,
his mothers watchful eyes
always on him.

As the tree grows older,
his trunk stronger
he sees the droughts and wars,
the pain and famine
that the world passes.

The now old tree
his heart is dying
his leaves show for the last time
the trunk grows weaker
until finally the dreaded day comes.
The day that will mean the end
the day that the tree falls
after 200 years of life.

Karen Dance (12)
Parkstone Grammar School

THE TREE

The tree stands tall,
Right up to the sky
And when the wind blows it is,
Shaking,
Swaying,
Rocking,
But as soon as the wind stops it is,
Statue like.

The tree is aware,
That autumn is here
And obliges by turning its leaves,
Ruby red,
Golden yellow,
Crisp brown,
So that the leaves can,
Flutter to the ground.

The tree is home,
To various birds
And beneath its canopy nestle,
Robins,
Blackbirds,
Woodpeckers,
Who always return to its sanctuary,
Of protective foliage.

Leanne Cave (12)
Parkstone Grammar School

CHANGES!

Autumn's now gone, leaves disappeared
Winter's coming, though not to be feared.

Crisp, glistening snowflakes fall to the icy ground,
One by one they float down not making a sound.
Covering the earth, a blanket of white
Robins in search for food with all their might.

It's snowing much harder now, you really feel the cold,
All animals hibernating, no baby fox to hold.

Winter's ruined everything, the trees, animal life and more.

At first it was beautiful, a wonderful sight to see,
But now I'm trapped, waiting to be set free.

The greys and blacks all around,
In the sky and on the grounds.

No more smiles on anyone's face
This cannot be the same place.

Open one then two eyes, waiting for the view
The grey dark sky no sparkling dew.

But wait I see a fox run by,
Some birds, robins with worms in the sky.

No dull snow trapping me
Just the sun saying, you're free.

Winter's gone and spring is here
Death has gone and life is near!

Lucy Sandford (12)
Parkstone Grammar School

THE SEA

In the deep the fishes roam,
A peaceful scene for all to see,
Although it's peaceful, it's a dangerous world,
Around every corner there could be trouble.

All of a sudden the fishes flee,
A monster is coming, a shark you see,
Eating his fill of fish and seaweed,
He came so quickly, no fish could flee.

But when he's full some fish come back,
But there is danger everywhere,
But no danger from people in this water,
It hasn't been invaded, yet.

Humans cannot come down here,
There is no air to breathe.
People have died down here,
They were caught in sinking ships.

The remains of these ships are on the bottom,
Covered in seaweed, rotting away.
Sad memories haunt the ships empty shells,
But these ships are now home to fish and coral.

But in this ship graveyard,
Sadness isn't present,
Lots of colour, is all around,
Out of all that sadness has come new life.

Shelley Richardson (13)
Parkstone Grammar School

DEATH

When will I die?
Tomorrow, the day after
Seconds away, decades away
When I'm least prepared
A newly born baby may crave the soul I have,
Given to me by another.

What will come upon me when I die?
Get lost on the way to heaven
Acquire the life of a ghost
Become a respected and admired star
Forced to create everyone's unpredictable dreams.

How will I know when I've gone?
Survey angels; detect devils in my ear
Sense a bizarre blankness ruling me
See it coming, and run for fear of failing.

How will our world survive?
Civilisation must learn to live together
Inventions and discoveries found deep in the minds of others.

What will death be like?
Light, dark, gay, oppressive, pleasant, petrifying

I will wait for these questions to answer themselves.

Rachel Schmieder (12)
Parkstone Grammar School

RAINDROPS

That must be her,
She has to come to take me home,
Can't be, Mother does not have ginger hair.

This could be her,
The one in the black car,
Maybe not.

It has been a week now,
I've spent hours here
Waiting at the window
Expecting her to appear.

Everyone is telling me
She's not here no more,
That she's gone up to that place in the sky,
Where Dad left to go in the war.

But I know she'll come some day
To rescue me from this place,
Overflowing with other children like me,
Each with their own special case.

My hands rest on the cold, flat window,
I count each raindrop as it falls,
One by one, my hopes are fading,
I am like a bird with no call.

Elizabeth Lever (13)
Parkstone Grammar School

FIRE

Blazing with anger, it cackles and screams
Destruction and despair, anger and hate
It longs for war, battle and violence
It rages with greed, self-pity and spite
Desiring injury, sickness and death.
In the black of night, it stands alone
But in fear and terror, it's loneliness shows
Its fork tongue lashes at unsuspecting souls
Who cannot stand the inferno of its heat.
Its furious hands share nightmares
But not just among children
Of running but not getting anywhere.
Of trying to scream, but no sound can emerge
But then with a hissing and crackling
The blinding colours of red, orange and yellow
Are gone.
The fire is dead,
What was once a furnace of evil,
Is now just ash.

Clare Hickman (12)
Parkstone Grammar School

THE TIGER

With stony marble eyes
The hunter creeps and prys.
With stripes that hide him well
He'll easily catch gazelle.

He catches his prey with ease,
Hiding in grass that sways in the breeze.
He digs his teeth in the flesh
Oh! What a terrible mess!

The poachers are on their way,
Please let him go, I pray.
I want to see him up
But if I did - he'd be poached.

His life is in terrible danger
From some cold-hearted stranger.
I wish they would leave him alone,
Not skin him to the bone.

Stephanie Butler (12)
Parkstone Grammar School

THE MIRROR

Mirror, mirror on my wall
In my bedroom she sees all.
Just sitting there she's all alone,
As if my cabinet is her throne.

As she sits she stares at me
And all that is around she sees.
She looks out the window,
She looks at my wall.
As if she's spectating
She's wisest of all.

What do you see?
She answers me
'I see your day, I see your life,
I see what you hate, I see what you like.
I can see the beauty that hides within
You can never lie to me,' says she.

Sarah Lings (12)
Parkstone Grammar School

THE LONELY JOURNEY

I fly through the mystical night sky,
Glistening with endless ease.
As I gaze down below,
I wonder if I just float on forever like a never finished dream.

Almost at once it stops,
Because now I see shapes forming beneath me.

I desperately try to think what they could be
And as the clouds begin to part,
Rooftops appear.

They look so similar when bunched together,
Their appearance like peas,
Squashed in spaces with no room to breathe.

I begin to feel lonely as time passes me by,
I want to call out and make it stop,
But time doesn't seem to hear.

Soon my journey will end
And I will fizzle away.
Soaring in the thought filled sky no longer.

Becky Sykes (12)
Parkstone Grammar School

WEATHER

Old women talk of the weather today.
The sun is shining, the sky is all blue.
Children play in the garden and pool.
Summer is now here and all is well.

The north wind now blows the leaves off the trees.
Clouds form in their stratus formations.
The rain pours down, turning to hailstones.
Autumn is now here and it is chilly.

Old Mr Frost touches the cold grass.
The snow flutters down and rests on the ground.
The children make snowmen with coal for eyes.
Winter is now here and it is freezing.

The cold seeps away, the garden warms up.
The women talk of the weather once more.
The clouds disperse and leave clear blue sky.
Spring is now here and it is warmer.

Helen Davey (13)
Parkstone Grammar School

TIGER KING

The water shimmered with my reflection
A duplicate of sheer perfection
My fiery colours
My snowy beard
Twelve foot of muscle
Admired and feared.
Compared with me
A lion's a wuss
And a panther's just
A big black puss.
I'm number one
I'm the best,
I'm the top
Above all the rest
They can't compete
They just don't understand
That I'm the king
Of all the land.

Laura Greany (12)
Parkstone Grammar School

THE WANDERER

As I travel through the desolate valley
As the harsh wind howls and cries
As the moon twinkles far away
I feel cold, lonely and afraid.

Tall, dark, murky forests
Cover the mountainous range
Holding me with their fierce stare.

My eyes observe every movement
As death throws his cape around me.
Shadows hide in every corner
And send cold shivers down my spine.

The elegant lady in the clouds,
Sweeps her silvery light.
With a calmness that strikes me
I gaze in wonder at her tranquillity.

How long will I travel and wander?
How long will no home greet me?
Well, the answer's in the stars . . .
I will wander until I'm given that purpose.

Sarah Nathaniel (12)
Parkstone Grammar School

CAPTIVATED BY FREEDOM, IMPRISONED BY LOVE

She stands and watches as the rain falls,
Magnified by the glass entrapment which surrenders her to abuse,
Showing a fresh world beyond her own,
Cool air against the pane of the glass,
Tempting her to nectar-sweet freedom.
Her hand reaches forward longing to touch,
And yet afraid. Afraid of angering her father,
Afraid of escaping her love and hate for him at once.

The rain continues to dance down the glass,
Joining hands before sliding onto the glistening sill.
The drops match her clear blue, weary eyes,
Her mind tormented.
How she longs to join them as they drop,
Free and clear.
Imprisoned in a house under lock and key,
Longing to explore, the fascinations of the world.
Captivated by freedom, imprisoned by love.

Cherilee Real (13)
Parkstone Grammar School

MIRRORS

I wake up in the morning
I look in the mirror
I ask my reflection
What will I be like?

> You'll be what you want,
> You'll do what you want,
> You may have your problems
> But you'll be all right.

What will I want?
What shall I do?
All through the problems
I don't know if I'll come through.

> Stop questioning yourself
> It may never happen
> And when it does, if it does
> Of course you'll come through.

Gemma Knill (13)
Parkstone Grammar School

THE TIGER

In the dead of night I prowl through the jungle
My orange and black stripes like scars from battles,
My bright and deadly eyes express my hunger,
I walk in the shadows well out of sight,
My tail swaying and my ears pricked high,
Quiet as a mouse, yet as big and heavy as a tank,
My big velvety paws pad along the ground,
Waiting and listening for any movement or sound,
Suddenly I hear a rustle and swiftly turn around
And see a gazelle walking towards me,
I crouch down low and watch my prey,
Ready to attack and catch my waiting dinner,
Then I pounce and catch the gazelle,
Perfect again just like every other day.

Mandy Toop (12)
Parkstone Grammar School

THE SEA

As the river flows in the sea,
The change is rather clear.
When the weather is wild and wintry,
The sea turns grey and deep, dark blue.
The waves crash savagely, violently.
Brutal to those who dare.
Calm - the sea is still tranquil
The wind has died down.
The sea is peaceful and quiet.
Soon, nightfall draws near.
Reds, oranges and yellows merge together.
The close of the day is here.

Manpreet Aujla (13)
Parkstone Grammar School

DAWN CASTLE

The trees stand tall against the blackened sky
The ground looks far below me
A wolf howls and stares at the moon so high
As I sit and wonder why? I sit here at night, so unafraid
As the spirits and ghosts of people long dead
Wail and glide below me.

As I look up towards the dawn
A castle seems to appear
I walk across the neatly kept lawn
As the night turns into morn, and the dark clouds drift away
The doors so big, glide slowly open
A great hall seems to appear.

The castle had stood dead for a thousand years
Laughter no longer filled it
No footsteps filled its long dark halls
As I explore - the lonely rooms, grow darker with each second
Until I see, an airy figure
A stained glass window behind it.

The room it starts to fill with light
The figure she turns to see me.
So silently she screams her fright
Then she looks out to the night, which seems to disappear
And slowly still, she seems to fade
And reach her arms towards me.

A flash of lightning fills the sky
A light, that seems to blind me
And as the light fades up on high
I find myself sitting, and wonder why
The castle faded, into the dawn
And the maiden called out towards me.

Becky Whing (12)
Parkstone Grammar School

ONE SINGLE WATER DROPLET

One single water droplet
travelled round the world.
Down violent whirlwind waterfalls
round placid mountain streams.

Calm and cool and tranquil
refreshing winter ice.
That single water droplet
swam beneath the ice.

Its passage was uncertain,
the ice began to melt.
Clearly speed was gathering
it turned a sparkling white.

That helpless little droplet,
tossed in the raging stream.
Danger lay ahead of it,
A wicked waterfall.

It tumbled, spun and spun,
landed in the freezing sea.
Evaporated by the sun,
to start life's cycle once again.

Hannah Gilbert (13)
Parkstone Grammar School

HATRED

The devil rules his fiery pit,
The heat unbearable.
He has set the twisting mind on fire,
Wild fire, that spreads throughout.

Madness, like the reddest berry,
The colours flashing, red, black.
The walls spinning faster,
A kaleidoscope of colour,
Red, black, red, black.
Forever . . .

Steph Sansome (12)
Parkstone Grammar School

WHEN DARKNESS

When the night was still
and the moon was full
and darkness fell upon the land,
they crept silent, hand in hand.

When the night was young
and the birds didn't sing,
and darkness fell upon the land,
they unlocked the door that barred their plans.

When the night was old
and the moon was fading
and darkness was leaving land,
they were away from the castle grounds.

When the night had faded
and the sun had risen
and darkness had gone from land,
they were away to their own special land.

When they awoke to find them gone,
a shadow appeared to warn them off
but darkness had taken the lovers-to-be
somewhere too special for you and me!

Jessie Jamieson (12)
Parkstone Grammar School

TIGER

In darkest night
With eyes alight
Sweeping through the trees
A tiger runs
Away from guns
As swiftly as the breeze
'Running, running
Must keep running
Get away from the terrible gunning
Dodge and dip'
From tail to tip
She quivers as she runs
And leaves behind the poachers
With the devastating guns.

Tegan Palmer (13)
Parkstone Grammar School

THE TIGER

Four legs have I, to run and bounce,
To creep and crawl, to leap, to pounce.
I have no friends to love and play
At the fear of danger, they run away.
I'm never hungry, too slick for that
I just wait and wait - till you turn your back.
I creep and crawl on the ground
Not making the smallest sound.
I sit among the dried-up grass
Waiting for the time to pass.
Four legs have I to run and bounce,
To creep and crawl, to leap, to pounce.

Kerry Shea (12)
Parkstone Grammar School

HORSE

He glides in the wind
Tail flying like a sail behind him.
Oblivious to all
Swallowing the ground
At a colossal rate.
Hooves pounding the turf.
He stops
Sides heaving
He turns his elegant head
He looks at you
With inquisitive eyes
Examining
Questioning
Then he turns
And canters away.

Charlotte Ferguson (12)
Parkstone Grammar School

THE OWL

An owls hoot, long and drawn,
like a flute sounds over the corn;
A harvest mouse, scuttling away,
had no idea it would be prey.
The owl swoops down to the ground,
one loud squeak then all is sound;
She is on her midnight flight,
and goes to sleep when all is light,
But when the night is here once more,
the owl is near as she was before.

Jessica Elkin (12)
Parkstone Grammar School

THE MIRROR

I am *she* with the silvery smile
I stand on the floor in the hall.
And though it seems strange
I can see for a mile
For I am *she* with the silvery smile.

I am *she* with the glistening heart
I tell no lies, just the truth.
I shine out like a light in the dark,
For I am *she* with the glistening heart.

I am *she* your secrets I keep
I'm always reflecting on you.
And though they are sad,
I never shall weep,
For I am *she* your secrets I keep.

Sían Horan (12)
Parkstone Grammar School

BLUEBELLS

A beautiful warm
Spring morning,
The forests alive with bluebells.

Surrounded by blankets of colour
And birds singing above.

White butterflies flutter by,
Lots of them are delicately hovering amongst the blue.

A beautiful
Spring morning,
The forests alive with bluebells.

Emily Bustard (13)
Parkstone Grammar School

My Mirror

I look in the mirror that hangs on my wall
and think and wonder as I stare, why wasn't I born tall?
Philippa, Sam, Georgina and Jo passed the teacher's height
long, long ago.
But still I stand at four foot three
and I know you'll always stand by me.

You'll help me feel tidy
when my clothes look bad
and help me with my hair
when it's frizzy and mad.

So get on with your commenting, contradicting and all
and help me look great . . . without looking tall!

Marianne Waite (12)
Parkstone Grammar School

Night

Night like a cloak covering the sun
plunging the Earth into complete darkness.
Black velvet sky.
Stars like crystals glistening
as the lights in the town fade, the night seems
darker, colder, more deadly.
Your breath, hot and steamy in the cold night air.
No comfort to be found, no warmth,
just cold icy air.
And just when you think your life is about to end
the cloak slips away.
Revealing a new day!

Naomi Makiola (12)
Parkstone Grammar School

Autumn

I am the autumn,
I will change the leaves to golden browns,
I will wrinkle them up like prunes.

I am the autumn,
I will make rain fall and the temperature drop
To make you shiver and shake.

I am the autumn,
I will rock the trees and strip them of their leaves,
Covering the floor like a carpet.

I am the autumn,
I bring ghosts and ghouls for Hallowe'en,
And fireworks that whizz and pop!

I am the autumn,
I bring the cold breeze with a wild imagination,
I make way for the winter.

Susi Berry (12)
Parkstone Grammar School

The Mirror

The mirror hangs on the wall all day,
hanging in a lonely sort of way,
you look at her,
she looks at you,
copying your every move.

I wonder what she thinks of me,
every day she must see,
the brushing of hair,
the brushing of teeth,
I wonder what she thinks of me.

The mirror hangs on the wall all day,
hanging in a lonely sort of way,
you look at her,
she looks at you,
copying your every move.

Laura Wicks (12)
Parkstone Grammar School

MIRROR

You'll never guess what I've seen
Over all these years?
Ageing faces, changing fashions,
Family, neighbours, smiles and tears.

Now Annie the eldest sister,
Goes out on Friday night.
You should see the layers of make-up,
Golly, what a sight!

Then there's our young Sophie
Who's into those Spice Girls,
She's Ginger, Posh and Sporty,
Doing little twirls!

There's mother with her lipstick,
Father with his comb
And Granny with her smartest hats,
You should have witnessed those!

They look at me every day
To check that they look OK
And if they don't, they stop awhile,
Until they're greeted with a smile!

Lucie Crew (12)
Parkstone Grammar School

LADY AUTUMN

Autumn raises her powerful hand
swiftly over the trees.
The trees raise their faces in sorrow
and begin to shed their leaves.
Crisp golden leaves fall like tears
to the ground,
Spreading a carpet of golden light
all around her.
The light of the moon shines on
autumn's face.
A smile appears in the empty space.
An empty space as white as milk,
expressionless as smooth as silk.
What pleasure she gets from sending
such pain to trees all around again
and again.
The trees stand there shaking and
shivering with cold.
Intimidated by autumn
but they try to stand bold.
Evil hearted autumn, cold-blooded
to the bone.
The trees keep on swaying afraid
and alone.
No one escapes from autumn's
cold eyes,
For she will find you and her
hand will rise.

Rachel Faulkner (12)
Parkstone Grammar School

Lady Autumn

Who makes the sun set
Colouring the sky?
Who tells the swallows
When it's time to fly?
Who makes the trees
Silhouetted in the evening sun?
I, Lady Autumn, makes every one.

Who makes the animals
All hide away?
Who makes it darker
At the end of the day?
Who gives the wind
A cold winter chill?
I, Lady Autumn, makes it all still.

Who makes the berries red,
Ripe, and sweet and plenty?
Who makes the nuts brown,
Small, and hard and many?
Who makes the harvest come,
The corn to stand tall?
I, Lady Autumn, makes it all.

I am Lady Autumn
My dress of golden leaves.
My hair of flowing chestnut locks,
I'm crowned as are the trees.
I make all of autumn
In all its splendour appear.
By far the most glorious season
Of all the year.

Amy Hebditch (12)
Parkstone Grammar School

I Am The Autumn

Summer has gone and now I am here
dressed in my golden gown.
My feminine ways are plain to see;
The warmth through the sun on the golden-
brown leaves.
And the devilish cold on the gentle breeze.

Throughout the time that I am here,
I see the birds fly south.
The trees grow bare as I grow old and
soon cruel winter will come.

He draws nearer and my strength starts
to fade,
As his icy breath fills the air.
But in my golden grave I'll wait
until my time has come,
I'll return to the birds,
and the trees growing bare -
I am the autumn!

Kay Holmes (13)
Parkstone Grammar School

Steam Train Stallion

Across the empty beach he flew like a steam train,
His coat, the colour of the coal feeding it.
His ears, like bits of metal being drawn back,
Held down to his head by an invisible magnet.

Two shining round stones lay in the side of his head,
Looking fixed and concentrated.
Fan-like nostrils flared out, the tail,
Party streamers hanging from the powerful body.

The constant sound of the drum hooves,
Crashing repeatedly on the wet sand,
Poetry in motion.
No mark of white on him.

The call from the sparkling ocean,
No longer a temptation to me as I sit alone.
Suddenly I realise the drum has stopped, the sea is calm,
The steam train stallion . . . gone.

Felicity Quick (13)
Parkstone Grammar School

THE MIRROR

I'm shiny, I sit on the wall
to show a reflection to all that look
into my wide ocean of glittering water,
they look as far as their eye can see,
out of the window and over the hills,
lakes, streams, trees and fields,
and ponder about the identical twin
of the world that lurks inside of me.
The image of the blood-red
whiplashed wall and the transparent
hole in the wall, known as the
window remains in my mind,
endlessly reminding me of how things
are and will always be,
until I am dislodged to a different life.
As the light begins to fade
I stay awake lonely and thinking
of the day ahead,
watching the stars twinkling in the moonlight.

Jodie Booth (12)
Parkstone Grammar School

Autumn

It's autumn time again with cold chilly mornings all dull and grey.
The leaves are turning brown after being green and healthy
all through summer and they are raining down on Earth.
The streets are littered with them, they're scattered all around.
The trees stand bare and shivering, watching as feet crunch upon
their clothes from summer as they are raked up and thrown away,
as the wind chases them around and around.

The days are short and cold and the nights are colder still.
Hot drinks are passed around as people huddle next to the fire,
glad of the warmth.
Shorts and T-shirts are put away, and the old woolly hats and
scarves are out again.
People breathe out smoke in the crisp cold mornings,
stamping their feet and jumping around to get warm.

Hallowe'en comes round, and ghosts, witches, wizards and pumpkins
run through the streets shouting 'Trick or Treat?'
Near the end, fireworks whizz by and burst and bonfires blaze,
lighting up the sky.

It's the end . . . and autumn gives way to winter.
With Christmas and New Year just around the corner.

Lauren Dyson (12)
Parkstone Grammar School

Sunset

The clouds entwined in a luminous band of red and gold,
The colours merging as one, bright bold.
The rooftops and mountains, piercing the sky,
Dotted randomly around the fields, gold ingots lie.

The road looks like sherbet and the trees are candy,
Everything shimmers, just fine and dandy.
Tomorrow's a new day, as the sun gives way to the stars.
If I can reach up and touch, then they'll be ours.

Susan De Lorey (12)
Parkstone Grammar School

BLACK AND WHITE

An old lady stands alone, defensive,
Her world black and white.
Living in a silent land,
Her house is her priority.
The smell of fresh bread
Mingles with the smell of diesel
Creeping in from the busy road outside.
She has nothing else left.
Her wrinkled face has seen most things,
People coming, people going.
Her memories of earlier life,
Flood back like tears.
Battles won and lost,
Friendships gained and ended.
Happiness overtakes the sadness,
But the sadness still hurts.
The gain of loved ones,
A fulfilling warmth.
The loss of loved ones,
A stabbing emptiness.
An old lady stands alone defensive,
Her world black and white.

Laura Annis (14)
Parkstone Grammar School

My Gran Sleeping

My gran,
Sleeping in her favourite chair.
I can't tell,
But maybe she is dreaming,
Or maybe just dozed off.
She seems happy,
What if she's sad?
Under that mask she wears,
Deep within her feelings.
She could be in pain,
What if she's hurt?
I won't think about that.
Memories,
Of when she was young,
Carefree and joyful,
Just like me now.

One day I'll be just like her,
Sleeping in that chair.
My grandchild will wonder about me,
I'm wondering about her now.

Bridget Keely (13)
Parkstone Grammar School

Yellow

The golden Labrador stretched out lazily on the sand,
The beach went on for miles,
Looking like a field of buttercups.
The blinding sun shone down like a spotlight in the sky.
Nearby a lemon ice lolly lay melting like runny butter,
Uneaten - dropped by some happy child.

Sophie Payne (12)
Parkstone Grammar School

SUNRISE

A fire burns the horizon,
A match lightly taps the corner of the sky.
The flames shoot across the corners of the world,
The black charcoal slowly dies away.

Beams shine through the smoke,
The world sits up in panic,
Edging further from the brightness,
Afraid for the new day.

The colours of the sky stand still
As a sweet blue extinguishes the flames.
The peaceful clouds lap the horizon
As a new day starts again.

Georgina Lang (12)
Parkstone Grammar School

AUTUMN

The leaves bronzed and crisp
stir with the wind.
As if waking from a deep sleep.
Then they lay lifeless again.
The cool breeze stirs the branches
of the silhouetted trees.
The sun going home for the night,
ready to rise early next morning.
Birds flutter to their roosts.
Getting darker earlier
All quiet,
apart from the owl and the mouse.
Then silence.

Laura Culham (13)
Parkstone Grammar School

Autumn

Autumn is here, colder than last,
As cold as the North Pole.
The wind blows and the golden leaves fall,
Leaving a sheet of gold covering the ground.
The trees look like bare bodies standing still,
Looking as cold as a snowman in the middle
                                   of the garden, all alone.
The conkers cover the ground,
Until the boy who comes every year, comes to collect them.
The squirrels get ready for hibernation,
Collecting all the acorns so they will have enough
                                   food until next year.
The frost starts to bite, so I wrap up warm
To protect myself from the cold.
Autumn's my favourite season, but winter's on its way.

Rebecca Lever (12)
Parkstone Grammar School

Raindrops

A lonely little girl
With a flow of golden curls
Counting the raindrops as they fall
She's listening to them speak
Can you here them?
Listen harder and be patient
Use your imagination
Try to fill the emptiness with their music
Touch the window and feel their dampness
Feel their drumming run down your spine
Can you hear them?

Hayley Morris (13)
Parkstone Grammar School

Autumn

She lurks in the atmosphere like a flying saucer,
Stripping trees bare with her power,
Causing some animals to hide and burrow,
She's like a two-faced witch showing both sides,
Creeping around the streets at night,
Hiding her face from any eyes' sight,
Invisibly picking the leaves off branches,
Littering them randomly on the outdoor floor,
Earning money for park keepers, slaving around,
                                    sweeping the ground,
Crops being harvested by the farmers and being
                                    sold to the factories,
Water pipes freezing after she casts the hazardous spell,
Giving plumbers the job of fixing those pipes.
I personally think she's a pretty lady,
But others think she brings ugly times, havoc and chaos.
She comes and goes like a prisoner on the run.
Each year she leaves us, we know she'll return.

Lauren Bridle (12)
Parkstone Grammar School

A Visit To The Dentist

The boy entered the big, scary, haunted house.
A ghostly voice called his name.
The dentist peered into the dark cave.
A flood of light poured in.
He tapped the icicles with his spear.
There was shiny water being reflected around the cave.
The light disappeared and there were clouds followed by rain.
A green coloured slime whooshed around the cave.
The cave went dark and the boy left the not so scary haunted house!

Hannah Jeneson (12)
Parkstone Grammar School

THOUGHTS RUN WILD

Float away, high in the sky, like a bird.
Run away, as fast as you can, like a cheetah.
Hide in the trees, protect yourself in a nest.
Hide in the long grass, like an ant.
Be free, as free as you've ever been.
Don't get captured, be careful.
Roam around, on the ground.
Land on the paper before you run wild.
Build up to a dramatic end.
Run wildly around the page.
Stop, you've finished, your job is done.
Captured, captured by a boy.
He's writing you for his homework.
It's the end, you're finished now!

Kelly Stark (13)
Parkstone Grammar School

TIGER

The tiger, ablaze with orange flames,
White hot around the throat,
Black burnt lines scarred onto its sides.
Moving, flowing, leaping,
Perfectly camouflaged against sun-bleached grasses.
Crouched, waiting, ready for its prey,
Swift gazelle or snack of antelope.
It pounces, lands, never misses.
Fills its stomach with warm meat,
Licks its platter sized paws.
Seeks the shadows, lays down its great head,
Shuts its amber eyes and sleeps.

Claire Sissons (12)
Parkstone Grammar School

THE BETTER MONTHS

October...

Noses flood with coldness,
While a red, orange and yellow rain falls.
Children pick up tiny hedgehogs
That have fallen from tall giants.
Creatures of an inhuman state disappear into the Earth.
While more creatures: goblins, ghosts and witches stampede the streets.
Cackling, laughing and crying 'Trick or Treat?'

November...

Thick walls of sound-eating monsters
Dampen the grass and air.
Cold fires dance and leap,
While stars sparkle on the end of sticks.
Dramatic increases of shooting stars fly and dart across the sky.
Large balls of cloth walk around,
Their only features, small red noses.

December...

Flakes of soap powder
That have bubbled over from the skies above, tumble.
Slippery glass forms from puddles.
Translucent cave decorations
Hang on window ledges.
City skylines of presents cluster around the tree.
Giant socks wait above a high fire.
And a fat, tubby man
Hands out gifts,
Granting all children's dreams.

Gemma Eastman (12)
Parkstone Grammar School

THE TREES

They started life as tiny green seeds,
Then little by little they grew into monstrous giants,
Waving their limbs as boisterously as boxers.

Winter fell and the trees threw a fantastic display of
Fire over their branches.
The envy was gone.

In spring they beamed like girls running along the shore.
We sang round the trees as the blooms flew off majestically.

The summers were interesting for the trees,
Their fruits grew like tennis balls hitting a wall in
Random directions and sticking.
As they fell, their pure juice poured out and the
Smell of fresh fruit wafted under our noses.

Sadly the trees grew old.
They had reproduced enough and it was time to pass away.
Their prune-like skin changed colour as they died,
Then the cycle of the seeds started over.

Sally Campion (13)
Parkstone Grammar School

AUTUMN RETURNS

Summer is fading and Lady Autumn slowly takes
to the floor once again.
She's dressed in fine woven gold silk and a dark
brown fur coat, sitting in her throne with a look
of authority over the world.

Trees gaze in despair as they see their lush
leaves turn from orange to brown and gently
flounce down to the Earth's floor.
Little animals scurry round getting organised
for winter's cold, arctic chill.

Young children enjoy conker fights and crunching in fallen leaves covered from head to toe in big bulky coats with woolly hats and multicoloured gloves. Hallowe'en is approaching, with pumpkin heads by the front door and witches and vampires every way you turn. 'Trick or Treat'.

The Lady of Autumn is growing weak and soon will no longer be able to hold off winter and so will saunter slowly back to her majestic cave in the sky to restore and rest for next year when she'll be back.

Sophie Clark (13)
Parkstone Grammar School

THE DANDELION

One dandelion solitary in a field,
Swaying slowly in the breeze,
When, suddenly, a gust of wind
Sends its seeds flying into the air.
Dancing above the treetops,
Wisps of grey float gracefully,
Gliding over hedges.
In the warm summer sun,
Birds twitter,
Bees hum.
The feathery seeds drift past
Chimneys and over roofs,
As they race through the withered
Leaves of a tree,
The wind dies down,
And the seeds float gently to the ground.

Jennifer Atkins (13)
Parkstone Grammar School

THE DANDELION

A dandelion stands proudly in a field,
Stalk green as grass,
Head white as snow.
She holds her seeds close to her,
Waiting for the perfect moment.

A slight breeze, scatters the infants,
Spreading them like confetti.
Floating like fairies,
Silently, sending wishes.
Delicate snowflakes dancing on the wind.

Transparent, fluffy and light,
Flying with elegant speed,
Tiny parachutes, bringing a new life,
Gracefully they begin to settle,
A new generation has begun.

Natasha Williams (14)
Parkstone Grammar School

ME

Inside me are my deepest, darkest secrets; no one will ever discover.
Below me are my feet, worn out because of the many miles
they have travelled.
Behind me are the good times and bad times; all memories, that I love.
Beneath me is the structure to which I belong; the world.
Outside of me is the air I breathe turning sour and polluted.
Across me are garments; silks, cottons and cat-like velvet.
Above me is the sunset, producing all the colours in the rainbow
in a cloudy haze.
Through me I am opaque, filled with air so I can stay alive.

Jessica Jarvis (13)
Parkstone Grammar School

WINTER MORNING

A bird sings softly in the cool morning air,
The dew glistens and sparkles on the grass,
The pink clouds are some far off world in the sky
And everything is peaceful.

An old, dry leaf drops slowly to the ground,
And the dog walker crushes it beneath her welly boots.
A pheasant flies over the hedge, flapping his wings
And lands clumsily on the other side.

The swans are still asleep on the river,
Their long, graceful necks tucked behind their silky wings.
The boats in the harbour float from side to side
And make the water ripple all around them.

A huge grey blanket hangs over the valley,
It is still and will not lift,
It chills you and makes you feel horrible
And you can't get it to go away.

The morning is a car with frost on the windscreen
And when you tip hot water on it
The steam monster rises from the deep
Because the air is so cold.

When your toes have turned to stones in your shoes
And your fingers become sticks in your gloves,
And your nose and your lips turn blue with cold,
You know that Jack Frost's been at work.

In the sky is the crescent of the moon,
Looking strange in the pale blue background.
In the east the sun is rising,
A golden ball warming and lighting the Earth.

Jessica Boize (12)
Parkstone Grammar School

08:15 Departure To Waterloo

Her young, unhappy face presses against the frosty, smooth glass,
Bitter rain drums on the roof and drips and splatters
Down the ticket office windowpane.
Outside in his neatly ironed suit
Her father waits expectantly for the creaking morning train
His polished shoes gleam on the platform side,
A hand holds a crumpled orange ticket to Waterloo
Watching the noisy train screech to a halt
Her eyes follow as he reluctantly boards
Buttons flash red
As the door glides open with a mechanical thud
Setting his briefcase on the bright blue seat,
He turns with a false smile,
Raising his hand, he waves.
The shining metal train slides from the station.
Her clear blue eyes dull with sadness,
Glisten with tears.
Time slips by,
Droplets of loneliness spill and slither down her already damp cheeks
As an ebony tide of despair washes over her,
She shuffles towards the door.

Clare King (13)
Parkstone Grammar School

Child In The Window

In a lone deserted street,
On a bleak winter's day,
See a girl behind a window
Counting raindrops, melted snow.

Feel the glass, cold as ice,
Smooth under the small child's hand.
Watch the raindrops glisten and sparkle
In the fading cold winter's sun.

The concentration on her face,
Her tiny fingers spread out wide.
Her eyes as deep as the deep-blue sea,
Staring out at the melting frost.

Her red woolly jumper,
Keeps her warm and safe,
As she gazes dreamily,
Staring into the mind of each raindrop.

Kate Kipling (13)
Parkstone Grammar School

THE HORSE

The horse galloped along the beach,
The cool waves snapping at his legs
And sand jumping out of the way of its huge hooves.
The horse's mane blew about in the gentle breeze
While the sun burned down on its hot toffee coat
As if trying to melt it away.

The horse swam in the cool blue ocean,
And jumped around in the frothing waves.
He rolled around in the golden sand
Letting the scorching heat of the sun dry him off.
He played amongst the swelling sand dunes
And the enchanting rock pools filled with mysterious
                                          creatures of the sea.

The horse rattled back and forth across the wide, flat beach.
Soon the sun began to set below the bright orange horizon.
The horse then started its last charge across the beach.
All you could see was the silhouette of the great horse
As it disappeared into the looming dusk.

Jessica Have (12)
Parkstone Grammar School

FROM WITHIN THE FIRE!

The knights, jousting in their long red robes,
Upon horses of brown skin.
They travel like flickers of light,
Their robes trailing behind them
As the Chinese dragon's tail trails behind its fierce face.
People's faces light up in anticipation
Some gasps can be heard within the crowd of people,
Above the crowd the cracking of whips is heard.
The smell of fury.
Steam rises from the horses' nostrils,
Smelling like smoke,
Biting at your nose,
And galloping about in your mouth.
Your throat feels swollen, dry and sore,
Burning, scorching hot.
Suddenly something has happened,
Both knights lie on the floor,
Blood pouring from wounds of war,
Burns of sorrow.
Their lives remain as ashes in the dark,
Cobbled streets.

Hayley Russell (13)
Parkstone Grammar School

WONDERS OF THE WORLD

Thoughts and pictures fill the air,
Half the people do not care.
They cannot see the detailed land,
They cannot hold it in their hand.

But if you only stop and look
In every cranny, every nook,
And stop and think about the land,
Then you can hold it in your hand.

The silver moon, the golden sun,
A land of mystery and fun.
It's not quite modern, not quite old,
Not scorching hot but not quite cold.

Rushing past you cannot see it,
If you stop then you can be it.
So stop and think about the land,
Then you can hold it in your hand.

Katie Smith (13)
Parkstone Grammar School

ILLUSIONS OF WINTER

It is cold. The air is shallow and sparse.
A cold, white desert of snow isolates me from the world.
The sun seems warm, but it is overpowered by the cold
                                            of the winter day.

I see a world of ice.
The fields are like a mass of sugar
Or the icing of a Christmas cake.

The fence is encased in ice.
It seems cold and hard like a prison gate.
The icicles like cold steel bars.
It keeps me separate from the outside world.

Suddenly, a ray of sun catches on the bars of ice.
They glow, warm and inviting, like a winter fire.

Then the sun is blocked.
The illusion, destroyed.

Michelle Cousins (13)
Parkstone Grammar School

SNOW

A cool, fresh morning,
Awoken by new falling snow.
Tumbling, like soft feathers, slowly to the ground.
I sit and watch them drifting past my window.

The wind whips round them,
Causing a great flurry of spiralling, whirling snowflakes
As the flakes persist, they become larger and heavier than before,
Covering the Earth's surface with a crisp, cool coating.

They start to shimmer as the sun begins to rise.
The wintry chill of the white crystals,
Slowly drenching the terrain before disappearing from view,
Leaving behind memories of a white landscape.

Emma Thompson (13)
Parkstone Grammar School

THE DANDELION

It stands there on its own, amongst the fresh grass,
Growing little by little every day.
As the wind blows the small seeds fly,
They come off the flower and into the air,
Millions of them float happily.
They spin gracefully as the wind takes them up high,
Dancing around in the sky.
When the wind soon dies down,
The greyish white seeds fall slowly,
They make a soft landing,
The seeds are scattered everywhere.
Another dandelion begins to grow,
It stands there on its own, amongst the fresh, green grass
Waiting to scatter its seeds.

Carissa de Souza (13)
Parkstone Grammar School

THE SEA

Another murder taking place over night; a helpless victim
                                        swamped by a giant,
Crashing and breaking down its defences first, then setting
its many pets to feed on the motionless bodies.
The shells washing through the sand, running, hurrying
                                        to the order of the sea,
Until the rage of the almighty fight is over.

A flock of hungry seagulls fill the bruised sky,
The sea has the right and power to knock over cliffs and houses and
no one can stop the mad battle of the enormous army.
The waves are like an extra springy Jack-in-the-box,
Jumping, jerking, sliding and gliding over the sharp rocks.

The scent of an angry animal looking for revenge,
A summer dream turned into a miserable nightmare,
The sea is moaning out and crying to any who will listen to its
                                        sincere cries of help,
Fierce, flaming like a red hot fire.

Then a new light is shone and ferocious beast is turned into gentle giant.
Smooth, soft, gentle music is heard,
Like a peaceful afternoon.
The shoreline had been moved by the power of the waves over the
                                        stormy night.

Nicola Wall (12)
Parkstone Grammar School

LIGHT

He raced over the hill, faster than sound, and back down the other side,
Cascading over the snow-topped mountains and imposing himself
                                                      on the landscape,
He skidded down a wooden valley and crossed a turbulent river,
                                                      which made it sparkle,
He could see a small, isolated village in the distance, awaiting him.
He heard a faint high-pitched alarm coming from one of the houses
                                                      in the village,
It flooded the previously silent hills and mountains, creating an
                                                      unnerving atmosphere.
He covered many miles at a time and his wings left nothing untouched,
As he closed in on the village, he looked back, but he was
                                        determined, nothing would stop him now.
He reached the first house and broke in through a shutter, that
                                            sheltered the window from him,
He slid through the keyhole and under all the closed doors,
As he did this, everything was left touched, yet untouched at
                                                      the same time,
He did not force an entry, so the family could do nothing.
He did the same to all the houses in the village and took nothing
                                                    and moved nothing,
He left the village with no regret, as if it was all in a day's work,
                                                      which it was,
He went onto the next village or town covering the countryside
                                                      in-between rapidly,
He knew his way and didn't hesitate once.
In the distance he saw his enemy, who was chasing after him, like
                                                      a dog after a cat,
He never caught his enemy either and has never faced him, he just
                                      knew that he brought a dark end to the day.

Rebecca Brickwood (13)
Parkstone Grammar School

SUNRISE

As light approaches, the birds start their dawn chorus.
From the darkness appears an orange, split open to splash its
                                                            juice around.
Above our heads, saddened boats floated across a dark, blue sea
                               like unpolished, disused silverware,
Now sunlight dapples on that blue, beautiful sea.
The queen of warmth and beauty once again touches her kingdom
                                                                     with light.
Wispy clouds, coloured pink, are spread across the sky,
Like pink ribbons to celebrate the sun's birthday.
The sun's light fills every space like a happy musical tune,
A tune which everyone hears and enjoys.
The taste of refreshing orange juice fills me with happiness.
Someone's blown a giant yellow bubble,
And it's floated into the sky.
Dancing yellow droplets have fallen and now they are spread
                                                               around the sky,
Like golden leaves fallen from trees in autumn.
The sun rising is a medication offered willingly and providing life
                                                                  for everything,
It's a contagious smile.
A yellow apple has been thrown into the sky by a giant,
A yellow Frisbee is spinning in the sky before falling back to Earth,
A sunflower has grown taller than any other,
Its gigantic bud opens up to a brand new day,
The sun has risen again, greeting me with its gentle, powerful light,
The sun is alive again, giving everything a bright burst of energy.

Rebekah Chadwick (12)
Parkstone Grammar School

Rainbow

Red is for a single loving rose in the middle of a bloodthirsty field,
With petals of silk and fur,
The stem of metal and hedgehog spikes.
A smell with the strength of stilton and deadliness of toxic waste.
Orange is a knife slicing through a juicy fruit.
The knife is a sharp blunt,
The fruit with a strong metal skin and paper innards.
When the orange water cascades over the metal, the room fills
with a sweet, genteel smell.
Yellow is a bumblebee floating gracefully round a pot of honey,
Fur of hard, soft qualities,
A sting made from an old rusty needle,
You know when one is near as they carry a tiny drill to attract
the attention of their prey.
Green is long grass running naturally in the wind,
It covers the world in a thick blanket,
Hard to protect yet soft to please.
All you hear is the blanket whistling to you faintly in the distance.
Blue are the curtains in the sky,
The cool, cotton fabric allows the Earth to breathe.
They close during day to give you warmth,
Then open at night to give you the glory of the planets.
Violet are the fluffy slippers on my feet.
The yielding texture against my toes,
So rich like velvet,
Reminding me of the smell of thick, creamy chocolate.

Holly Sibley (13)
Parkstone Grammar School

REACTIONS

A broken frame on a sun-cracked morning,
Gnarled limbs against the sky,
A broken window, carved by age,
Forbidden roots, desert dry.

Parched claws, sparse and spare,
Where no bare feet may run,
Muddy scratches, and mossy patches,
Beaten by the afternoon sun.

In winter months, the rain does drown,
Old man, from root to tip,
A safe harbour for tired souls,
An immovable Noah's ship.

The grass is drenched, and blunt,
Trampled by a thousand feet,
Marked with soles, on ground now blind,
Left longing for the heat.

Samantha Wynn-Adams (13)
Parkstone Grammar School

WINTER

The world is a blanket
Of white, as far as sea,
The rumbling rattles the hills all night,
The red-breasted robin in the snow-covered tree.

The wind is a lion roaring at twilight,
The coldness is death beckoning me,
The daylight bring heat from the blanketed world,
The morning, like a flower, has now uncurled.

Sarah Belcher (12)
Parkstone Grammar School

SUNRISE, SUNSET

It starts as blue as the deep depths of the ocean,
Engulfing it to reveal the pinky orange of the
mysterious monsters that live there.

Later evolving into a devilish red,
The colour of blood, as if day has been killed to
make way for night.

Following the vampires in flight, making their
way to people's fright,
Comes the panther-black sky,
Moving slickly and smoothly through time and space,
As if sleep was a race against time.

Slowly, like a whale yawning to greet the new day,
The sky opens exposing an opaque morning blue.

Watch out world, I've woken up!

Zoe Hyett (12)
Parkstone Grammar School

FIRE

A furnace surrounded me last night,
The blistering heat, the immense flame.
Dancing lively, gleaming brightly,
Crackling, spitting, blazing with heat.

As I sat reading, the heat was scorching,
Rain was falling from my face and hands.
And as I continued I found myself in an ocean
Of saline water, up to my knees.

The room was ignited and was next to the sun,
I was in an oven, being cooked alive.
It was filled with sunflowers, roses and orange poppies,
Expanding in size from ant to an elephant.

At dusk it was time to wade through the ocean,
To stop the blaze and bring back a chill.
The flames were so huge that it took a stampede
To put them out and leave the black embers to burn.

Lynsey Treharne (13)
Parkstone Grammar School

THE SKY

The sky is a rainbow of colours,
A wonderful sea of land.

The friendly, dancing clouds way up high, on the smiling
summer's day.
The purple bruised sky before the monster of a thunderstorm;
biting, snapping and tearing the sky apart.
The thin, slim clouds that whiz about, on a windy day,
like bullets shooting out of a gun.
The most beautiful and colourful sky is just before the sun sets a
blend of peach, pink and yellow.
The regal dark blue and black night sky, is studded with glimmering
stars, like diamonds on royal blue velvet.

The sky is a rainbow of colours,
A wonderful sea of land.

Ellena Humphries (12)
Parkstone Grammar School

THE STORM

It started off as a few clicks,
Then it became a little bit more rapid.
Suddenly the barrier dropped
Like a speeding arrow.
The clicks became more like loud thuds
And later those thuds turned into heavy
Elephants falling from the sky.
It was like the sea was dropping from outer space
Onto our tiny little planet.
Then it came,
The terrible noise that made the ground shake,
A major earthquake.
A golden thread of electricity zapped our world
Making its hair stick up on end.
Suddenly it reached its crescendo
And slowly burned out,
Leaving a trail of destruction behind.

Stephanie Jones (12)
Parkstone Grammar School

THE CHASE

As she ran, the glacier slid
Back and forth on her arm.
The ground rumbled,
As if the pounding of her feet
Had caused the earth to vibrate
Like an earthquake.
Great waves of hair tossed from side to side,
Like trees being thrown about in the wind.

The forest bellows behind her,
Howling in the distance,
As if the resident king of beasts,
Had decided this is the night for the ultimate kill.
The sky was covered with a blanket of soot,
Getting blacker, then blood-red.

Lizzie Paddick (12)
Parkstone Grammar School

IN THE NIGHT

A chill is in the air tonight,
Only the scrambling of the foxes can be heard,
Like children fighting over their toys.
The trees rustle, a secret being told.
Then silence.

One single firework goes off, disturbing the silence,
A car door is slammed, an engine is revved up
While another firework goes off.
As the noise of the engine fades away,
The eerie silence screams out.

More rustling as a lonesome squirrel climbs around the trees,
A thief in the night.
An acorn drops onto the ground near my seat on the swing.
The wind rustles through the trees,
A whisper in the darkness.

As I look up, I see the stars,
Small specks of glitter
Stuck on a background of the deepest blue.
The high-pitched squeaks of a bat are heard
And the haunting calls of an owl.
A chill is in the air tonight.

Carita Challands (12)
Parkstone Grammar School

FROZEN

Frost covered my window sill.
I peered past the small icicles that had formed on
                              the eaves of my house,
A cold mist hung over the carpet of snow that covered the ground,
Cold fingers of air crept through the cracks in the window frame,
They whipped through my hair like freezing ice cubes
                              rubbing over my body.
I crept down the silent stairs of the dreaming house,
Down in the eerie kitchen I turned the icy tap,
Only a trickle of freezing water seeped out.
I shivered.
A draught of cold air and several sparkling snowflakes were floating
                              in from the slightly open window,
I battled against the wind, reaching for the window latch,
I looked out, more icy snowflakes drifted from the dull, bleak sky,
Silence surround me as I walked back up the cold steps to bed.

Lauren Darby (12)
Parkstone Grammar School

BUBBLE BATH

The mountains rise out of the clear, closed-in sea,
Growing rapidly,
Taller, taller, faster, faster,
Then suddenly stops.

There is a soft sound,
A sound that no one can describe,
The mountains are as white as snow and feel like silk,
They stand out like a fluorescent ball in a white landscape,

But slowly they start sinking,
Sinking and swirling into the now murky depths,
Slowly, slowly down the black hole,
Now long forgotten.

Polly Smith (12)
Parkstone Grammar School

RAIN

The fairies have been crying,
Their sad teardrops patting the white waves.
They sound scared now,
Are they running away?

The rain is faster now,
The gnomes are coming.
They're chasing the fairies away,
I can hear their loud footsteps.

Next came the giants,
Thundering along,
In their big leather boots,
Shouting for the gnomes and fairies to surrender.

What do they want?
They've scared us into our homes,
Their flashing eyes slashing into the darkness,
They've gone over our heads, their footsteps fading into the distance.

The gnomes and fairies come out of hiding,
And quickly run away,
Scared of the giant's force,
The fairies have been crying.

Margaret Goymer (12)
Parkstone Grammar School

THE WAYS OF FIRE

The colours, bright and bold,
So bright, must close my eyes,
It's burning inside me, I must keep away.
The heat is burning,
Toasting my skin,
Al I feel is,
Pain, pain, pain.
It boils the blood.
All I see is the light,
Flames spitting, sizzling,
Biting at my skin.

The blazing sight has burnt my eyes,
Smoke, choking me.
A burning sensation in the throat,
The killing pain!

Andrea Holmes (12)
Parkstone Grammar School

THE GHOST HORSE

Flying past like the breeze of winter,
Distant pounding, heartbeats racing,
Heavy breathing down your neck.
Eerie shadows under the silver moon,
Strange shapes flatten the grass,
You know it's there but you just can't see it.
Graceful and elegant is the shape,
Strong, with more power than any man's weight.
Then suddenly I see it, standing tall,
Beautiful - the most amazing thing I've ever seen.

Katie Merchant (12)
Parkstone Grammar School

WATER BABIES

Drip, drip,
Trickle, trickle,
Plop, plop,
Splash!
Cold droplets of life,
Hatch out,
Parachute down,
Land,
And slide away.
Drip, drip,
Trickle, trickle,
Plop, plop,
Splash!
Cascading down,
Towards their hard, metal world,
Far below,
Where the liquids play.
Drip, drip,
Trick, trickle,
Plop, plop,
Splash!
Life is one long stream of bubbles,
To the drips and drops of the tap,
The tap, the tap.
Drip, drip,
Trickle, trickle,
Plop, plop,
Splash!

Emma Jane Waring (12)
Parkstone Grammar School

FIRE

I watch on in amazement at the
Beautiful, yet deadly flames
Licking at the bark of the tree.
All I hear is the crackling of the wood
Swirling around and around my head
As if it would never stop.
I watch until all that is left is the
Coal-black cinders and ash, as the
Flames move on to engulf another innocent tree.
The deadly, grey, billowing smoke is making my
eyes shine with tears.
The smell is killing me,
It is suffocating me, but still I look on.
Hypnotised by the reds and oranges dancing against
the lifeless, empty night sky.

Sarah Lonsdale (12)
Parkstone Grammar School

NIGHT CHILD

The sky a black jackdaw, wings outspread,
Slowly creeping across the world,
Vast sheets of darkness scattered with diamonds,
Some tinted with scarlet, turquoise,
I walk through the loneliness, everything
With a new place.
Big bass drums pound against my ribcage.
Like a fish, faced with a shark
My life turns around.

Strange, unknown creatures swirl
With the mist.
My heart longs to leave,
The loneliness unbearable
I long,
I pine
For the clock strike
Of dawn.

Melissa Hards (13)
Parkstone Grammar School

STORM

The lightning flashed like a camera,
Close to us, its yellow streaks like
Blonde hair. The rain pounding onto
The ground like smashing mugs.

The wind howling like dogs,
Darting around like a ray of light that has
Just hit a hall of mirrors.
Then the thunder hit us, like a shuddering earthquake.

The house would tremble in its own fear.
The fire went out as the rain gushed down the chimney,
At the time, the house was a terrifying box of horrors,
Unleashed and roaming round.

Giant's feet a-stomping, golden streaks appearing,
The howling of the dogs, the pounding of the rain.
It was a terrifying experience destined to happen again.

Clash! All the lights in the house went out.
Like an instant eclipse, to make the movement more unpleasurable.
The house lives on, the storm will come again.

Lucy Moseley (12)
Parkstone Grammar School

STORM

Soot-black clouds gather in the sky,
Casting a shadow over the village and
An eerie silence creeps in,
Filling the spaces around it.

Small drops of rain fall graciously
To the ground below, like leaves falling from a tree.
The quiet pitter-patter of the drops is soothing,
Like a lullaby sung to a small child.

A strong wind blows through the meadow
Whining like a pitiful horse and
The old cottage gate creaks open and shut
While in the distance the leaves on the ground rustle noisily.

The rain, now wet and watery, continues on
And attacks the ground like a marching army.
It batters the cottage roof aggressively
And creates a deafening sound until . . .

. . . The rain dies down and stops.
. . . The wind calms to a gentle breeze.
. . . The clouds depart and the sky turns blue.
. . . And once again the sun comes out.

Rosanagh Besley (12)
Parkstone Grammar School

MY NEW FRIEND

I sit like a statue upon my bed.
I take a look out of my window.
I see the blackness of the sky being
Pierced with luminous yellow needles.

I feel the rumbling of distant thunder.
I see the streets filling with silver rain.
I see houses with no light, just curtains.

I go downstairs and open the thick, heavy, wooden door.
I walk slowly down the empty streets of loneliness.
I come across two sorrowful eyes pleading through the darkness

With wet dripping fur,
Shivering in the cold
But a friendly lick and a wagging tail
Gave me inner warmth on that cold winter's night.

Gemma McCready (12)
Parkstone Grammar School

SEASONS

Spring has come with small bouncy balls
Trailing with buds of cotton wool.
Coloured hairs sprout from a green scalp.
Little suns scurry around. A blue sheet
With small, white fluffy cushions cosy on the horizon.

Summer scorches the bodies lying on a
sheep's back, the exploding heat bomb
In the sky boils the sphere we call Earth.

Autumn falls and a paintbox blasts
To the trees, rat-like things scurry the streets,
And swirling streams of fish cover the grounds,
Then dying and crumpled up orange, red
And brown seals the land.

Winter comes and minute clouds fall
From the sky. Crystals everywhere and
Polar bear bite makes one cry a
Puddle of frozen tears.

Kelly Taylor (13)
Parkstone Grammar School

THE ORANGE TREE

The man climbed up the tree,
Just like a creeper, twisting and coiling round.
He worked his way up for the treasure,
Like a snake constricting its prey.

He scrambled higher and higher,
To reach the orange gems.
The man looked like a monkey swinging in the trees,
But all his intention was to provide for loved ones.

Finally he reached the rich fruit,
Delicious and juicy and also fresh.
Fresh, like bathing in a relaxing waterfall,
The man took what was needed and travelled home.

All that was left of the tree was leaves,
It was bare . . .

Harriet Archer (12)
Parkstone Grammar School

THUNDERSTORM

Tiny wet splodges gathered on the cabin,
An all night attack of pittings and pattings.
Man all the portholes, board up the doors
Just like hell's fiery,
We're at war!

The eyes blew in of the house where I was born
I demolished the chimney to survive this great storm.
The tent in my garden collapsed like a chair,
Great Zeus had just thrown a bolt in the air!

The piercing pinlight blinded my eyes.
I bumped into books, chairs,
Plates of silver in colour.
All of these broke like an ornament under cover.
My cabin had broken like my heart in a shudder!

Helen Gardner (12)
Parkstone Grammar School

THE MOODS OF THE SEA

Another darkened night,
Hear the wolves howl among the dogs scrapping
To the last crash and bash.
Morning rises,
The piano plays, the keys of the wonders of music
Flowing into your mind.
Hear the dolphins bring in peace and harmony.
Night has fallen once again but rats are scurrying
As wind is picking up.
The night feels more anger tonight,
As dragons burn up blazing fires.
The piano plays low keys as wind is picking up even more.
Peaceful moods fill with hatred of such fierce animals.
The sun rises, the fire is blown out.
All is calm once again.
Pianos are back in tune and not so shallow.
The animals are within the sea as the sea is within the animals.

Lauren Orchard (12)
Parkstone Grammar School

BUBBA MOONSHINE

Bubba Moonshine is an amazing cat,
His coat, as black as night,
His eyes, they sparkle like the stars,
His eyes, they sparkle bright.
He cares not for gravity as he floats up in the air,
When he is lost in space he fills out his questionnaire.

Bubba Moonshine is a spectacular cat,
He travels to the stars,
He's been to every planet, Saturn, Jupiter, even Mars,
They say that he is crazy to travel oh so far,
He cares little for what they say,
He's been to Achernar.

Bubba Moonshine is a contented cat,
He sees his family twice a year
And brings them each a case of beer,
But for his mum he brings back,
Chocolate moon cheese bars
And plenty of rock from the planet Mars.

Bubba Moonshine is a daring cat,
As he shoots above the cars,
He flies past the Moon
And stops on Mars,
He needs to refuel,
Before he travels to the stars.

Bubba Moonshine is an astronaut cat,
But he is no common moggy,
His face, smart and clean,
Fur, he does preen,
His tail is like a flagpole,
It sticks up straight in the air, so I say to you once more,
Bubba Moonshine is an astronaut cat.

Heather Marchment (12)
Parkstone Grammar School

WINTER'S WRATH

The wind cracks like a fine bone China goblet, frozen by
                                                  winter's touch.
The snowflakes individual faces stare blankly, as they gracefully
Glide swiftly down to Earth, resting upon a serene white ocean of light
Heavy feet of lead crush once tranquil snowflakes into one another,
Turning them into nothing but another part of that white ocean.
The trees' blank faces look solemn as they swing and grab out at me,
While a sky of cotton wool pink bares the delicate flashes of ice.
Just ice and only flakes, that land upon my finger when I hold it out
To them, and watch as the flake, the individual snowflake
                                                  turns to water.
A small droplet, I look out over the ocean white that will soon turn,
Into that, water, individual water hidden and cannot see,
As it soaks into the ground drop by drop, till gone.

Kim Smith (12)
Parkstone Grammar School

THE DRAGON

Lost beneath the earth for a thousand years,
Like an acorn, dormant for so long,
But ready to explode with life at any moment.
Coated in a fine, dust-like layer of leavers.

The moonlight shimmers, picking out faint glimmers
Of light from its dry, blood-coloured scales.
It lets out a breath, like a boiling geyser
And snorts out a skein of hot, misty sulphur.

Its mouth, a subterranean cavern filled with stalactites,
Inhabited by a monster serpent, which tentatively tastes the air,
Sends messages to the deep, dark realms of its stomach,
Like a bottomless pit, full of boiling lava.

How long has this huge monster lain here?
Since the days of knights and conquests,
Or since the dawn of our blue, green world?
How long will it sleep for, a hundred years, a thousand?

Let us hope that this primitive lizard-like creature
Has not come for us yet,
With blazing eyes and scorching flame,
And knife-like teeth to rip and rend.

We can only pray that it will lie asleep
For another long, hard thousand years,
That it will awaken hungry, angry,
At the end of the world, at the end of life.

Liz Ford (12)
Parkstone Grammar School

SUMMER

A sweltering heat settles on the earth,
As a dragon sleeps on his bed of fiery gold,
His scales glimmering like jewelled shells
On the sands of clear blue sea,
Whispering the secrets of the ocean.

Down between the honey-coloured sand dunes,
Among the grasses, picnics and delicious treats
Display themselves under the eye of heaven,
And through the dusty, salty haze,
Children wrestle and play in the sands
Like young bear cubs.

Under a rusty sky,
Fields of wheat grow as golden as a lion's mane,
And in the strawberry patch,
Beads of water glisten on their tender flesh,
Like the eyes of fairies,
Their colour, as rich as the devil's blood.

Along the side of the dusty roads,
Sunflowers nod their heads dozily
Under the slowly disappearing sun,
Her sunbeams kissing the horizon,
As she peacefully returns to her slumber.

Clare Sepping (12)
Parkstone Grammar School

Autumn

The sun's rays burst through the oak's golden canopy.
Looking out of my window, I see the frozen lakes
                        which border my street.
The windswept leaves like hungry, scuttling rats, follow
                        the Pied Piper leading them,
Over, under, round and through obstacles.
As the ice queen fills the air with her cold, frosty breath,
The ships, still and silent, anchor themselves into the
                        golden carpet of stubble.

Sian Swift (12)
Parkstone Grammar School

The Harbour

The evening sun watched over the harbour,
Like a firefly it hovered,
Soaking the harbour in its radiant light.
The still water lethargically rippled,
As a lone yacht unwillingly moved along.

The town was falling asleep
Under the warm glow of the dying sun.
One by one lights flicked on,
And then in time off again.

The sun rolled down the sky
And gave a stream of red light
As the darkness rushed upon the town.
The black knight ruled supreme.

Christopher Howard (13)
Poole Grammar School

The Millennium

The lights were bright,
The sky, deep blue.
Fireworks were roaring,
The crowd were too.

'One minute left!' I heard someone shout,
I felt a sudden chill.
The new millennium was coming,
It was 40 seconds 'til.

I gazed out of the window,
All the beauty I could see.
It made me feel excited,
Opportunity.

Everyone was dancing,
The bells started ringing.
I smiled and joined the crowd,
Now everyone was singing.

But something was not right,
Nothing much had changed.
Everyone was happy,
But I felt much the same.

It was all over-hyped I thought,
Looking out to see.
But everything looked wonderful,
And that was good enough for me.

David Loader (13)
Poole Grammar School

THE BALLAD OF THE TAMWORTH TWO

Once there were two young piggys,
Who were stubby and round,
Who fancied an adventure,
So escaped from the piggy pound!

They busted out on a Tuesday,
From the back of a van,
The driver spotted them too late,
As down the road they ran!

They scrounged around in litter bins,
For the next couple of days,
They really wished for nicer food,
But there were no other ways.

But then they were spotted,
By an old man from Cork,
They only just got away,
From becoming some roast pork!

They decided to visit the farmyard,
Where they had been born,
But they'd have to find it quick,
As their scent was still quite warm.

As they were coming to the farmyard,
They were seen by the farmer's mate,
They tried to make a run for it,
But this time they were too late!

They were taken back to the abattoir,
By the farmer's men
But before they went under the butcher's knife,
They went and escaped again!

Once again there were two young piggys,
Who were still stubby and round
Who again fancied an adventure,
Who escaped again from the piggy pound.

Oliver Williams (13)
Poole Grammar School

POOLE HARBOUR

The water ripples, and is heaved into the harbour walls,
The pungent waste of bitter alcohol floats past,
From the pub around the corner,
The seaweed strangles itself in the salty water,
And is then combed free by the current.
All is silent.

Suddenly, a heavy tugboat smashes the calmness,
The air is coated by thick lashings of smog and
Defenceless water is crushed into the harbour walls,
Making the other boats groan and sway.
A smell of smoke chokes your throat and eyes are squinting.
The seaweed darts, tangles and goes nowhere but into itself.
The bridge lifts and shuts, the tug is gone.

The small waves send themselves back to sleep,
The warm air and comfortable smells return.
The seaweed flows loosely and effortlessly once again,
And finally, the red sun sparkles the water as it sinks
Behind the horizon, and the harbour closes its eyelids.

Michael Bannard (13)
Poole Grammar School

THE DREADED AUNTEATER

A strange man once lived
His name was Peter
His job was strange too
He studied anteaters.

Once a specimen was found
That puzzled poor old Peter
Because there was one big difference
It was more of an aunteater.

It had eaten seven hundred aunts
Across the USA.
It might have been seven thousand
It's really hard to say.

One day Peter thought he'd try
And catch this terrible beast
He'd mount its head on a wall
And eat it as a feast.

Peter set out one weekend
With a gun, lawnmower and net
The aunteater was hiding in Canada
But ran at this terrible threat.

Peter could see it in the distance
With an aunt hanging out of its jaws
Peter then caught up with it
The aunteater bared its sharp claws.

Peter pulled his gun from his trouser pocket
But, alas, it had gone
He did still have the lawnmower
So he turned it on.

Peter pushed it over the aunteater
Who gave a tremendous squeal
Peter smiled with amusing glee
For it was now Peter's meal.

Peter carried it home on his back
Put the aunteater's head on the wall
Turned the oven on gas mark 5
And then ate its legs, tail and all.

Tim Matthews (12)
Poole Grammar School

THE FORESTS

The grey streak of the road,
Cuts through the green splendour of the forest,
The trees, shimmering in the gentle breeze,
But through this, a grey choking smog,
Drifts through and creeps along the soft, damp leaves.
Then men with strange tools that roar,
Come and destroy the forest,
And grey, faceless buildings are built.
To build another hive,
For the fast metal boxes on wheels,
And yet more trees are felled,
For paper, blank, white sheets,
Which have no life, no meaning.
The green blankets of trees are shrinking.
And humans are the pests,
That will be wiped out,
By nothing but their own selves.

Vincent Geoghegan (13)
Poole Grammar School

THE LITTLE LION

One fine day in the jungle
A little lion cub was born
With his bright bristled fur
And teeth as sharp as thorns

He played alone in the jungle
Having fun I suppose
He nosily sniffed a hedgehog
And hurt his small damp nose

They became the best of friends
They went everywhere together
They climbed up small trees
And went hiding in all the heather

But one hot, dusty day in the jungle
An elephant came along
He nearly trod on the small hedgehog
But the lion shouted 'Be-gone'

Soon the hedgehog grew old
His spikes fell to the ground of stone
And now in the large green jungle
The lion walks on alone.

Daniel Wallbridge (12)
Poole Grammar School

LOST IN THE SANDS

Golden as the sands around it,
The Lost City lay buried in an oven.
Silent and still,
Deserted and dead,
The city had lain lonely for many years.

Beneath the desert sands,
The city held memories of prosperity and wealth,
Yet, all had been lost to the strength and power of nature.
Who knew when it would be released from its prison of heat?
Or was it buried in its grave awaiting a funeral . . .

Peter Hodges (13)
Poole Grammar School

THE CITY

The city
With its bright lights shining
And its traffic buzzing
And everyone eating take-aways
(Indian)

The city
With its skyline filled with stone
Its streets and pavements full
Every crisp packet scavenged through
And every little rat seeking a home.

The city
With its fake market stalls
Its shopping malls packed
And people from every race and country.

The city
At day, a place of work
At night, a blaze of colour
These are the ways of the city.

Ben Priest (13)
Poole Grammar School

NIGHT PARTY

The sun goes down
The sky turns red,
Night time is coming
It's time for bed.

We close our eyes,
And go to sleep
But then outside
A boy hears a peep

He gets out of bed
And out of the house
And there on the ground
Sits a wee little mouse

He goes to the mouse
And pats it on the head
Then he goes back upstairs
Back into his bed

He hears another noise
Below on the ground
Goes over to the window
And sees a foxhound

As he watched these animals
He was able to see
That more animals were coming.
How many more can there be?

Out of the shadows
All the animals come.
Until the garden's full
A party has begun!

As the animals play
The sun starts to rise
The cockerel crows his cry
And the noise dies . . .

Joe Abreu (12)
Poole Grammar School

THE STALKER

At night a silent predator stalks,
Eyes burning like coals reflect the silvery moon.
Ears pricked for the slightest sound,
Eager anticipation of a tasty meal.
A rustle attracts instant attention,
The cat's body flows into a silent crouch.
The claws extend in preparation,
Every muscle is taut, ready to pounce.
Edging forward towards its prey,
One giant leap is all it takes,
For the victim to be caught.

Daylight slowly emerges,
The sun begins to rise.
The prey locked in the jaws of the cat,
A trophy for its beloved owner.
The warm glow of the indoor fire,
A loving lap awaits its arrival.
Last night's hunt is soon forgotten,
And sleep soon takes over . . .

Jonathan Morse (13)
Poole Grammar School

When People Came

The oak trees had stood, for a hundred long years,
And the birds singing was beautiful and music to the ears,
The trees were shimmering in a rusty haze,
And mice were scuttling through a tree root maze.

Then people came and disrupted the peace,
And the mighty oaks went tumbling with ease.
The dozers and diggers, started with a roar,
And the bushes and shrubs, down they tore.

The chestnuts and beeches, at them they hacked,
And over the tree roots went the tracks.
The rain began to pour, spit and then dribble,
And the workmen drove on, relentless and miserable.

The trees and the mice and the bushes have gone,
And where there was forest, there is brick and stone.
The people have destroyed something that they can't replace.
And this is a fact they will eventually have to face.

Stephen Moore (13)
Poole Grammar School

Forest Poem

The forest had such wondrous trees
With bright green luscious leaves.
Red, blue, purple and green
The flowers were so supreme.

The forest had such great activity
All the animals were so frisky.
Pigs, woodpeckers, ants and bees
Were all dancing in the lovely breeze.

The sunlight hit the forest so bright
It filled it with such gorgeous light.
It made all the flowers bloom
It got rid of all the gloom.

It's such a wondrous place
To see it in all its grace.
It makes you feel so good
Yet it never will be understood.

William Hanmer-Lloyd (13)
Poole Grammar School

THE HOLE IN THE WORLD

Puff, puff, puff go the industries of our world,
Throwing smog and fumes way into our sky,
Like an old man puffing from his pipe,
Whatever happens to this gloomy mass of gas.

'Protect our Earth,' shout the protesters,
'Save our planet,' say the politicians,
'Where are our fish?' wail the animals,
What causes these dreadful happenings?

Up goes the gas,
Way up into the sky until it reaches the outer covering,
Gradually burning its way through like an angry dragon,
Until it permanently scars this shield forever.

Max Walker (14)
Poole Grammar School

RED

Red is the sunset in the afternoon,
And ghastly medicine on the doctor's spoon,
The face of a tired mother
After a long time at birth,
The laughter of the devil,
As people face death.
Red is a rag
Faced with a bull,
Also a syringe with blood so full,
The danger of an explorer,
And the breast of a robin,
The sweet smell of cherries,
Such agony with sunburn,
The Red Arrows as they leave Hurn.
Albinos with their gleaming eye,
School vests running by,
The deafening sound of a sigh.
A Ferrari,
And poisonous snakes on safari,
The warmth of the sun,
When the day is done.

Matthew Revill (12)
Poole Grammar School

TYGER, TYGER

Tyger, tyger burning bright,
Only trees within his sight,
The thud of feet, grows louder and louder,
And then we meet.

Eye to eye, head to head,
I see him, he sees me,
To him I'm dinner,
What do I do?

Do I shoot him and risk my life?
Or do I run and leave him to his business?
Who knows? Who cares?
I'll shoot him.

With my shotgun at the ready,
I aim, I'm ready . . . I pull the trigger . . .
Bang the piercing crack rips through the forest,
Like thunder through the sky.

Is he dead?
I don't know.
I hear a rustle
I spin round . . .

Tyger, tyger burning bright,
Only trees within his sight,
He gets to his lair, in the middle of the night . . .
And starts dinner.

Stephen Worth (12)
Poole Grammar School

FIRE ARROW

The firecrest is a tiny bird.
But its feathers are made of fire.
Everywhere to have its tune heard.
Is its only melodic desire.

He looks around with a golden eye.
Like the sun on a deep blue sea.
As he trails it lazily across the sky
And drapes it on the tree.

He flies around on a quest for food.
And stops to eat some cherries.
Though his table manners are crude
He gets the linden berries.

He flies through branches as he sings
Though the gaps be small and narrow.
He flashes on with flaming wings.
Straight and fast as a feathered arrow.

Daniel Ambrose (13)
Poole Grammar School

WOLVES

Sharpened fangs, his coat a greyish hue.
Fresh eyes found as china blue.
His mind and spirit of braveness be,
The youngest cub. How handsome he.

Mothering instincts I find as true,
The she-wolf guards her litter new.
And father returns his brood to feed,
Maintains the line in wolf pack breed.

Natalie MacDonald (11)
St Leonard's Middle School, Blandford Forum

MYSTICAL TOWERS

I walked forth to
Two big doors,
Which I reached out
With my little paws.
I turned the handle
As gentle as can be,
I opened the door
And along came a rug in front of me.
I swiftly said, 'Hello'
And looked around the room,
Down the stairs came a shadow
With a loud boom!
The room was filled
With a warm look,
Lots of things
And more than one book.
I walked through
The big room
Watching the shadow
Facing my doom.
Along walked a lady
With a smile on her face.
'Hello' she said 'this is my place!'
I walked to the stairs and met the lady dressed in jewels,
We sat by the fire whilst talking
About what we admire.

Kaylee Hawley (11)
St Leonard's Middle School, Blandford Forum

INDIANS

I imagine that I'm an Indian, who rides on the plains in the Wild West,
Where I hunt buffalo to eat and to use to dress.
In the daylight I ride around on my horse in the desert,
And at night I watch the moon turn into a crescent.
The bison I can hear, so I get ready with my spear,
Then when it hits them like a lightning bolt, they have a surprising jolt.
We care for our world and look after it well,
With lovely sights and beautiful smells.
The sun comes up upon the horizon,
Shining its light on the bears, buffaloes and bison.
I live in a tepee surrounded by others,
My father, brother, sister and mother.
We tell stories of our adventures all through the night,
About dancing, singing and cowboy fights.
We enjoy riding on horses and look after their foals,
And doing religious dances around totem poles.
When the moon and stars come up to play,
We realise it's the end of the day.
That's what I imagine an Indian's life was like.

Andrew James (11)
St Leonard's Middle School, Blandford Forum

THE WEATHER POEM

The beautiful sun shines all day,
Over the mountains we all play,
The sun shines all the way,
As we pray the sun will stay.

I wiped my hand across my windowpane,
I felt a cold chill in the air,
I looked out my window, the frost was here again,
The white frost covered the trees and ground.

The rain fell down pitter-patter on my windowpane,
We wanted to play outside,
So we jumped up and down in the rain,
But still it rained.

Snow fell down,
It was very cold,
So we all frowned,
We made snowmen in the snow.

Claire Stickley (11)
St Leonard's Middle School, Blandford Forum

THE RAIN

Everything is soaking
down in the woods today.
Spiderwebs hang with a
silver tint.

All night long
came the gushing sound of
the dripping,
dropping rain.

The birds fall for their young ones
as the rain patters down until
it hits the floor with
a great big splash!

Everything is glimmering with
water droplets which
have landed on them.

Everything is wet in the
woods today and that's
the way I like it!

Natasha Cox (12)
St Leonard's Middle School, Blandford Forum

My Grandfather

The grass parted beneath my grandfather's feet,
Beads of sweat dripped off his forehead
and onto the bridge of his nose.
His shirt clung to his mighty back
as he lugged the logs up the hill
and into the snug warmth of the sheep shed.

As the door of the shed creaks shut
a sheep nuzzles into his thigh.
He hears a soft bleating of a newborn lamb
come from the pen in the corner.
My grandfather picks him up in his huge hands
and gently places him down outside the pen.

My grandfather takes a warm bottle of milk
and holds it in front of the lamb's mouth.
The lamb suckles immediately on the bottle end,
Gulping down the liquid inside.
When the bottle is empty my grandfather picks up the lamb
and places him back in the pen.

Now my grandfather is no longer here,
His death brought great sorrow.
But one day I will see him again,
Not so long from now.
On that day I will laugh
with my grandfather again.

Sam Goudie (12)
St Leonard's Middle School, Blandford Forum

Forget Me Not

Forget me not,
Forget me never,
Think of me, I'm yours forever.

On a mountain,
Up a hill,
Wherever you are
I'm with you still.

Staying with you
Day and night,
When the moon's
Low or when it's bright.

Like a panther,
Like a bear,
Never mind
I'm always there.

Natasha Strevens (11)
St Leonard's Middle School, Blandford Forum

Christmas Mail

The post arrives, I rush to the gate,
I'm expecting a parcel unless it's late.
The postman slams his van door shut,
And hands me the bundle that I immediately cut.
It is nearly Christmas so there are lots of cards,
There is also my parcel, it is quite large.
The date on the package is for the twenty-fifth of the twelfth,
I shake and squash, what is this great wealth?
I cannot guess, I must wait
Until Christmas Day, early not late.

Henny Clarke-Hall (13)
Sherborne School For Girls

The Tiger (King Of The Forest)

The tiger roams, where no man goes,
In the deepest forest that sees no snows.
He rules the kingdom, is head of his pack,
He wanders away leaving no track.
Meandering through the closest trees,
The air is still, there's hardly a breeze.
There's a menacing feel floating around,
Silence is threatening, you can hear not a sound.

The light is falling, the shadows appear
In the eerie twilight you can feel a fear.
Of something quite deadly, something mean,
The atmosphere's growing but nothing's been seen.
The tiger he turns, goes back through the trees,
The atmosphere breaks, the forest is free.
And the danger is over, but not for long,
He will return, powerful and strong.
Holding the forest in a terrible fear,
Not knowing when, he'll next appear,
Creeping stealthily along the ground,
Never making the tiniest sound.

Katharine Jacob (13)
Sherborne School For Girls

The Beach

Down the silky sand,
Which is tickling my feet,
Leaving perfect footprints,
Skipping down the beach.

The crystal water lapping on my feet
With its rhythmic comings and goings,
Watch tiny crabs scuttle away,
So natural but yet fantastic.

Floating on my back bobbing up and down,
The sun gently kisses the water,
Over dazzling reefs,
I leisurely paddle back.

Back on the silky sand,
It's tickling my feet,
Leaving perfect footprints,
On my quickly warming feet.

Sophie Byrne (12)
Sherborne School For Girls

THE VULNERABLE MOUSE

He scuttles somewhat nervously
Through the crispy, dry layer hiding him,
The universe overhead holds many dangers for him.
The most dangerous only warns
By a silent bird's wing.

He's feeding for a family, one with many young,
He can't hunt for long, he's got to hurry.
His field's in danger of harvesting,
But he takes his time
In case someone notices his mime.

He scuttles to the blackberry bush,
The birds have already had it.
He's in luck, he found one on the ground,
He runs and snatches it as though it's a race,
But someone's spotted his mime.

Caroline Franklin (12)
Sherborne School For Girls

WAR

In the morning I open my door,
I can smell the distinct smell of war,
I can see destruction and fear
And the crack of guns is all I can hear.
Bombs are rushing down from the sky,
Shrieking screams as people die.
The fear is pulsing through my veins,
People soaring in aeroplanes.
Ships steaming in from out to sea,
My mother comes calling for me.
The air raid siren wails in the night
And everyone feels a tingling of fright.
Running downstairs for the cellar door,
Opening softly and lying still on the floor.
My father's bravely fighting for his life,
Trying desperately to end this trouble and strife.
After hours and hours of suspense and fear
I am scared and shaken like a frightened deer.
My mother soothes me and I feel upset,
I wish I lived in a country that war has never met.
I hope that all of this fear and death shall end,
But I know it will take forever for people's bad ways to mend.

Lizzy Lillington (11)
Sherborne School For Girls

A RIDDLE

I rise in the east,
I set in the west,
Below me I see the countryside,
Animals play and munch green pasture,
People sing the song of God,
Green, green, green galore.

I rise in the east,
I set in the west,
Below me I see tall towers but no flowers,
No animals, no happy song,
But the bustle of busy workers,
Dull, grey but no green as before.

Fenella Kerr (12)
Sherborne School For Girls

AT NIGHT, A DREAM...

Floats...
    as in a breeze,
    like a boat on the seas.

Flies...
    very high,
    like a star in the sky.

Drifts...
    like a cloud away,
    to come back another day.

Sees...
    you sleeping in your bed,
    creeps, slowly, pops into your head.

The dream has come and now is here,
dream on sweetly, feel no fear.

Charlotte Carlton (12)
Sherborne School For Girls

THE SWAN

The swan is graceful, gliding,
Across the lake, almost sliding.

Neck up, to look so good,
Elegant with a crisp white hood.

Not a feather from its place,
Perfect position, just like lace.

Gathering up a lot of speed,
Which soon (of course) she'll use and need.

She takes off, leaves the ground,
Is soon high up, to where she's bound.

She won't come 'till next year.
Will she have such beauty, 'tis what we fear?

Sarah Hatherell (12)
Sherborne School For Girls

THE WOLF

Deep, deep, deep down in a wood,
lived a girl called Little Miss Riding Hood.
One day she thought she'd take a snack
to her little ol' grandma's 'lovely' shack.
So off she went hop, skip and jump,
until she met a wolf with a thumping bump.
'Oi!' said Hood, 'you big bully, you!'
'I'm not freeing you, till you tell me where your going to!'
'Let me go, I'm not telling you!'
So off she went with a click of her shoe.
'I know where she's going' said the wolf, suspecting gran.
So off, zoooom! He ran and ran.

Later that day the wolf entered the shack,
In bed lay gran, beside her a sack.
The wolf eyed both but then held back.
'If I put her in a sack she might get away.'
Then suddenly he remembered he hadn't eaten all day.
Slowly and silently he crept to the bed,
quickly and shockingly he bit off her head.
The rest of the body I'll save for my eats,
so carefully and cunningly he got in the sheets.
'And then,' he said feeling content and good.
'I'll just wait here for Little Miss Riding Hood.'

Amy Mayhew (12)
Sherborne School For Girls

PRECIOUS WAR PONY

Trotting pony, thundering past,
Howling through by the English mast.
A horse who's brave
And fights for the knight.

Tiring, slowing, feeling down,
Steadier walking down to the mound.
A horse who's weak
And tired from the cannon screams.

Little pony collapsing to the ground,
Men all floundering round and round.
'Little pony stay awake,
You'll soon be in your field by the lake.'

Lucy Stewart-Richardson (12)
Sherborne School For Girls

Rubbish

Rubbish, rubbish it's everywhere,
People nowadays just don't care.
Crisp packets, coke cans and sticky chewing gum,
It looks just like a revolting old slum.

If we don't stop, wildlife will die
And the next generation will say, why? Why? Why?
A few centuries later the world will be clean
But if we don't start now that won't be seen.

So put your rubbish in the bin
And then you won't have done a sin.
The next generation will have space to play,
Let's clean the world right now, today.

Eleanor Wilson (11)
Sherborne School For Girls

Holiday Panic

Sun cream, shorts and cricket bat,
camera, T-shirt and straw hat,
goggles, flippers and swimsuit,
bucket, spades, shoes and boots.

All packed up and in the car,
full of petrol, going far,
to dogs and cats we say goodbye,
time is short, we've got to fly.

Down the motorway we hare,
and reach the ferry with seconds to spare,
to find the tickets we're unable,
we left them on the kitchen table.

Harriet Crabb (13)
Sherborne School For Girls

MY PROJECT

Oh no, my project is due today,
I haven't done it! What will I say?
I am a ghost, my pen nib broke,
I am the Queen, look here's my cloak.

My house blew up, my room caught fire,
Honest Miss, I'm not a liar.
My collie dog, she had a pup,
She needed food, she ate it up.

The house was burgled, (I stood tense),
The police needed it for evidence,
When the burglars came, they took a lot,
Alright, I confess, I actually forgot.

Kate Boughey (12)
Sherborne School For Girls

IMAGINATION

Branches droop from their lordly master,
The storming wind tossing them from side to side,
Garbage cans tip their heads in admiration
as the wind puffs gently by,
Pebbles are thrown in all directions
as a great roaring monster rushes past,
The little maples are brushed to one side
as the wind sweeps past.
The wind is playing chase with the leaves
that dart away on their toes.

Harriet Gabbey (13)
Sherborne School For Girls

FLU JABS

'One, two, three, four people to go!'
This time in ten minutes it would be over.
'Next' called the nurse.
'Good luck, Charlotte,' I whispered
and the door shut.
A horrible silence crept down the corridor,
My back shuddered.

I will never forget the annual feeling
you get on 'flu jab' day,
Like statues we all leant against the wall,
Our eyes glued to the door.
And ears pricked like mice,
Ready and waiting
for the word that meant so much, *'next'!*

The distinct smell of TCP hovered in the air,
The door creaked open,
Charlotte edged her way out, Rosanna trotted in,
Like the press we questioned her, poor Charlotte.

All too soon the time had come,
I walked in and rolled up my shirt sleeve,
My muscles were tense.
'Right Katie.'
She took hold of my shaking arm.
I looked out of the window.
'All done, have a sweet dear.'
'Really!'
'Well that was easy!'

Katie Grimshaw (13)
Sherborne School For Girls

THE SLEEPING, THE WAKING, THE SLEEPING AGAIN

All is so quiet,
The world is at rest,
The sun doesn't shine,
The stars are at their best,
The night sky is clear,
The moon shines down upon
                his kingdom so near.

The darkness is so deep
But yet so divine,
As the night sky awakens
To reveal its secret wonders.

Birds' song breaks through,
People begin to stir,
Doors and windows fly open,
The morning dawns once more.

The sun shines brightly overhead,
The treetops blow in the wind.

The sun shines to and fro,
In the busy city below,
On and on the world goes round
Doing the same old thing.

Then the pace of life slows down,
The evening draws once more,
People go into their homes and
Darkness falls once more.

Sara Gledhill (13)
Sherborne School For Girls

The Sun

The rays of light enfold the world,
And sets the world on fire.
It unfurls its blanket from the surface,
And slowly but surely retires.

As the ball of light
Emerges from the horizon,
The blanket is swept across the world,
And for twelve hours shines on.

It is now dark,
The glowing ball has gone.
No longer are we happy,
The shining has shone.

Rebecca Wicker (13)
Sherborne School For Girls

The Coming Of Winter

I opened the front door,
The freezing cold air hit my warm body like thousands of needles.
As I breathed out my breath looked like the smoke from a puffing dragon.
My feet felt like blocks of ice,
My fingers turned blue,
I knew that winter was nigh.

Jessica Filbey (13)
Sherborne School For Girls

GHOST

It was a cold, dark winter's night,
I knew something would give me a fright,
The stairs creaked, a wind blew,
The windows rattled, no birds flew,
I heard a scream, I looked around,
All went silent, there wasn't a sound.

I got out of bed and opened my door,
There was a note upon my floor,
I picked it up and carefully read
That soon I was going to be with the dead,
I heard a scream, I looked around,
All went silent, there wasn't a sound.

I walked down the stairs, in the pitch black,
I was getting scared, should I turn back?
I decided against it, so I continued down,
Oh I wished I had put on my dressing gown,
I heard a scream, I looked around,
All went silent, there wasn't a sound.

The stairs ended, 'At last,' I cried,
All I wanted to do was to run and hide,
So that's what I did until I found
Myself tripping over a gigantic mound,
I heard a scream, I looked around,
All went silent, there wasn't a sound.

I picked myself up and realised that
It was only my fat tabby cat,
I thought I had had enough for one night,
Until I was given another fright,
I turned around and what did I see?
The hall mirror and no reflection of me!

Jemima Lofts (13)
Sherborne School For Girls

The Train

The train goes endlessly on -
Like a metal snake,
Hissing and slithering across the land,
Across fields and bridges, valleys and ridges,
The snake continues,
On and on,
Past rivers and lakes,
Towns and villages,
Houses and farms,
Slithering onwards,
Puffing and hissing across the land,
Past walkers with dogs, marshes and bogs,
The snake continues,
Up and down,
Past factories and cities,
Shops and offices,
Forests and ponds,
Slithering onwards,
Hissing and lumbering across the land,
Into tunnels,
Through stations,
Past signals and hedges and steep rocky ledges,
Over and under,
Past cattle and horses,
Churches and pubs,
Schools and gardens,
Slithering onwards,
Hissing and steaming across the land,
The snake continues,

The sun glints on the restraining metal rails,
The train wants to be free,
To go on and on, over and under, up and down,
Forever.

Jack Pritchard (12)
Sturminster Newton High School

THE OVERSIZED T-SHIRT

The oversized T-shirt in which nothing can fit,
Inside burns a fire which has never been lit.
Engulfed by its emptiness enticed by its charms
the oversized T-shirt covers more than the arms,
(the hands, the legs, the feet).

Untouched it remains in the package it came,
Never sought after, feeling much dafter,
Surrounded by taunts and cruel, evil laughter.
Feeling unwanted and so out of place,
Its conscience is haunted, mental scars on his face.

So it's left just to dream
of hem-lines and seams
(the miracle of sewing machines).

Manufactured at home
by a nan all alone
with a tape measure that's hard to read.
The oversized T-shirt
cotton by breed lives
hoping one day to fit in with other tops
and the joy that each one gives.

Gavin Blackhall (14)
Sturminster Newton High School

THE WATCH

A watch is a bomb,
It waits to explode.
A wheel that is spinning,
Slowly on.

The long narrow painting,
With colours so bright,
Fixes wheels within wheels,
To my wrist.

The face is the sea,
With the sun shining down,
Reflecting and glinting,
Golden.

This building site,
Has rods being lifted,
Into exact positions,
Of time.

Ian Lyster (12)
Sturminster Newton High School

WARNING - PARENTS ABOUT

There are two very common words
In the language of teenagers,
Which happen to be . . .
'I'm grounded.'
Parents just can't see
How torturous this is,
To make us stay in the house . . .
For what seems an eternity!

Then there's the fact that they don't like your friends,
They're either too common,
Or too polite.
When it comes to parents
You just can't win.
So I'd chuck the whole concept of the idea,
In the bin!

Natalie Snook (13)
Sturminster Newton High School

WHALE

It is an earthquake with earth exploding in
different directions of a whale splashing in the sea.

It is a zebra galloping with swirling black
and white colours.

It is an enormous mountain with clouds gliding
past as it swims through the sea.

It is a beautiful sea of wild flowers,
blowing side to side like the waves of a whale.

It is a deep puddle with lots of creatures.
The splash of a welly boot, and a whale 'jumping'
and splashing in the sea.

It is a fountain squirting with water as the whale
bursts out water from its blow hole.

It is an enormous bouncy ball bouncing into the sea.
A whale jumping high.

Tiffiny Errington (12)
Sturminster Newton High School

WEATHER

Weather is like a dice, you never know what you will get.
It has different things like the sun:
The sun is like being in a hot oven, it is like a ball floating in the sky,
It lights up like a light bulb.
But then there is rain, it is like having a cold shower,
It is like a little pat on your back when it hits you,
It can be hard and hits you like stones.
Then there's hail, which hits you like rocks.
Then you have thunder and lightning that is like a beat of a drum,
Like a flash of heaven.
The snow is like a big sheet that covers part of the world,
It's like having a cold, you shake and sneeze all the time.
The rainbow has colours as bright as a child at birth.
Rainbows are never-ending like a hard day at work and like a desert.
Floods would be like being as small as an ant swimming for life.
Then it all ends, like us we have to die like parts of the weather.

Michelle Dennett (13)
Sturminster Newton High School

THE DOLPHIN

It is a jumping Jack-in-the-box, jumping up and down,
To show off its wonderful dance to the others.

It is a dodgem dodging in his little car,
Dodging the other dodgems and crashing.

It is a shiny, smooth frog just hopped out of the water,
When you pick it up it has a smooth, wet tummy and back.

It is a deep sea going mad as it hops about and makes waves.

It is rain freshly out of the cloud and into the deep blue sea.

Terri-Marie Bugler (12)
Sturminster Newton High School

THE FIVE SORROWS OF WINTER

The first sorrow of winter
Is the quietness all around,
The birds flown off for the emigrating season,
The foxes scanning greedily for their prey
Disappearing into their holes with disappointment and fury,
The heads of other animals peeping out of the opening of their refuge.

The second sorrow of winter
Is the pond freezing over,
The frogs hopping away from their home,
The birds skating along the ice
Leaving scratch marks
And carefully avoiding the weak parts.

The third sorrow of winter
Is the freezing frost
Carpeting the land for miles around.
The frost freezing on the windscreens
Waiting for its enemy to come and scratch him off,
Its coldness dominating the early morning air.

The fourth sorrow of winter
Is the bare fields,
No cattle to liven them up;
The water troughs stand unused,
The only animals that can stand the cold
Are the sheep that live on the hills.

The fifth sorrow of winter
Is the cold and dark
That prevents people going outdoors,
The children losing the long evenings to play,
Children unable to play outside
Because of coughs and sniffles.

Sarah Gray (13)
Sturminster Newton High School

THE FIVE JOYS OF WINTER

The first joy of winter
Is the snow
Falling, covering the land
With a white, soft sheet.

The second joy
Is Christmas,
The excitement of waiting.
Then eyes widen and mouths drop
As the child pulls out two shiny pennies
From the bottom of her sack.

And the third joy
Is the trees
All dressed up
In silver, gold
And a fairy floating on top.

The fourth joy
Is the decorations
Hanging from the walls
That inspire people
And making them happy and welcome.

And the last joy
Is the new year.
Everybody ready to count down from ten,
Waiting to see
What the new year will bring.

Kelly Dowding (12)
Sturminster Newton High School

THE SIX JOYS OF SUMMER . . .

The first joy of summer
Is the smell of the atmosphere,
The scent of the red strawberries
And the succulent raspberries.

The second joy of summer
Is the glorious, crystal blue sky
With some occasional pure white
Fluffy, cottonwool clouds,
Floating by.

The third joy of summer
Is the golden yellow sand,
With the waves lapping on the shore,
As hoards of people
Slowly invade the beach.

The fourth joy of summer
Is the heat from the sun,
Directing its powerful rays
Down on the scorched earth,
From a ball of red fire, high in the sky.

The fifth joy of summer
Is the sensational ice-cream,
Which you slowly lick
And then enjoy the cool sensation
Slowly gliding down your throat.

The sixth joy of summer
Is the beautiful colours of a butterfly's
Delicate wings, as it distantly flutters around
Amongst the busy bees,
As they make their sweet pure honey.

Keeley Brand (12)
Sturminster Newton High School